LETTERS

Mr. Sedg[...]
Lord [...] [...]
not accepted.
1788

James Manning

or

[...]bez Bowen Esqr.

Providence

LETTERS

from the Corporation of Brown University

Lives of Usefulness and Reputation

1764 – 2023

Edited by LAUREN ZALAZNICK

BROWN

Produced by Disruption Books

For information about special discounts for bulk purchases, please contact Disruption Books at info@disruptionbooks.com.

An excerpt from *The Marriage Plot* by Jeffrey Eugenides appears courtesy of the author.

Every reasonable effort has been made to obtain permissions and supply complete and correct credits; if there are errors or omissions, please contact Disruption Books at info@disruptionbooks.com so that necessary corrections can be reflected in any subsequent edition.

Cover and book design by Sheila Parr

Printed in Canada.

ISBN: 978-1-63331-098-8

First Edition

This book is dedicated to students, everywhere.

———————

We can't know someone's story until they share it.
And until we listen.

Contents

Most sincerely do I wish that the Institution under your
patronage may receive the smiles of indulgent Heaven; while
you as individuals rejoice in the labour of your hand.

—REVEREND JOHN STANFORD

Honorary Master of Arts, 1788
Trustee, 1787 – 1789

Editor's Preface

BY LAUREN ZALAZNICK

THE CORPORATION OF BROWN University comprises forty-two trustees and twelve fellows. As the institution's governing body, it oversees Brown's policies and strategic plans in order to advance the University's mission. Brown's core ambition, which many take as a mandate, was written into the preamble of the University Charter of 1764:

> Institutions for liberal education are highly beneficial to society . . . preserving in the community a succession of [students] duly qualified for discharging the offices of life with usefulness and reputation . . .

Most Corporation members speak of the extraordinary sense of humility and fulfillment that comes with this responsibility. It's quite a lofty goal.

There are almost 120,000 alumni past and present but only about 700 current and former trustees and fellows. So it's not surprising that many students, alumni, parents, and even faculty have the impression of a somewhat opaque (mysterious at best, intimidating at worst) body of old, privileged people, mostly white, mostly male. I certainly harbored that perception the day I walked into my first meeting in the fall of 2011.

Part of the purpose of this book is to tell the story of how my perception changed and why that matters.

Each time the fifty-four members come together for a meeting, the group sits in what is known as the Corporation Room, a stately space on the third floor of University Hall, the first building erected at Brown, in 1770. Originally, trustees and fellows were appointed for life. Over time, term limits were established. Since 1944 trustees (and fellows since 1981) have been required to submit letters of resignation.

On Friday, May 22, 2015, I was finishing the fourth year of my six-year term. The tradition is that the Secretary of the Corporation reads each letter aloud at the spring meeting on the eve of Commencement Weekend. As usual, the letters were utterly enjoyable. Some were notable for their wistful elegance, sense of history, or wit. The next letter began. I started to feel a sense of heightened emotion. It was devastatingly personal. Was it just me? I looked around the dignified room. From recent alums to CEOs of major corporations, I saw teary eyes and heard muffled sniffles. This letter was from a person I had known and admired for nearly thirty years. Yet I had never listened to his *story*.

I had a flash of an idea: these letters deserved to be read, the stories *heard*, by others. As the readings continued, I began to visualize a patchwork quilt. Each letter was beautiful on its own, but when stitched together a remarkable image of Brown's significance in a changing world emerged.

In May 2017 I heard my own resignation letter read aloud. The meeting adjourned, and we all scattered. My conviction that Brown's story should be told in this way remained unshaken, but the urgency receded as work and life kept up their mighty pace.

For all the wrong reasons, I finally had some time on my hands during the dark days of the Covid-19 pandemic. Jolted by the social, political, and racial reckoning in the spring of 2020, my brain was aching. Amid the debilitating disharmony, I struggled to think of a time when people with disparate worldviews could even communicate, let alone unite, around a common cause. I thought of my time on the Corporation. Its fifty-four members have utterly distinct backgrounds, yet they converse with respect and congeniality even when confronting the thorniest of topics. Prioritizing their commitment to Brown, they represent mutually held values driven by a shared ethos.

It was time to bring the book to life.

I had my first call with Brown's president, Christina H. Paxson, in late June 2020. I tried to communicate the goals of the book: how the resignation letters reflect the country's social, cultural, and political transformations; that the letters embody human stories that deserved to be disseminated more widely than the select group of people who hear them behind closed doors each year; that we had a responsibility to build bridges to the current generation of students, not widen gaps. I was concerned that I had plenty of enthusiasm yet not enough "evidence" for the president, an esteemed academician, widely published economist, and legendary data hound. To my good fortune, she and Chancellor Samuel M. Mencoff embraced the idea—or at least the passion behind it.

I realized I didn't have even the most basic information: How many letters were there? How far back did they go? And *where were they*?

Catherine Pincince, Senior Associate Secretary of the Corporation, and Russell Carey, Executive Vice President for Planning and Policy, would become the University's shepherds of the project. Even during the pandemic shutdown, Catherine started to unearth letters from filing cabinets, computer files, storage boxes, and who knows what other nooks and crannies of the campus. Over the span of months, her sleuthing yielded an abundance of iPhone snapshots, low-resolution scans, and faded faxes delivered in tranches to my inbox.

Somewhat overwhelmed, I created a database of names, resignation dates, graduation dates, concentrations (what Brown calls academic majors), and notable biographical facts. I was uncovering a chronology of progress. There were many "firsts." Among them, the first female, Black, Asian, Hispanic, and internationally born trustees, fellows, and officers joined the Corporation. I read references to academic and social upheavals of each era. It was exciting to see personal attestations that reflected when and how the seeds of change were planted.

Somewhat late in the editorial process, I received nineteen resignation letters from the archive at Brown's John Hay library, spanning 1785 to 1804. Each one is a beautiful historical artifact. Though their laborious calligraphy and handmade envelopes sealed with red wax seem like a distant relative of our dashed-off emails and frantic texts, the content of their letters reveals some surprising connections. Apparently, founding Corporation member Edward Upham kept missing the meetings because he never got the invitation. A couple of centuries ago, he did what many of us still do today—he blamed the post office:

> The notices were "Caryed to Northampton and was there neare 2 months before it came to hand . . . when it shold have been Superscribed, Westspringfield [sic]," Massachusetts, an insurmountable twenty miles away.

As I read and reread the letters, certain themes began to emerge. Trustees and fellows frequently reflected on the differences between the cultural era of their undergraduate years and that of their Corporation tenure. A mid-1970s graduate confessed that the first thing she thought at her initial Corporation meeting was that she "was now officially part of the establishment and not on the outside of University Hall protesting some earth-shattering issues." It was nearly impossible for one fellow to believe that he "had finally become one of 'them.'"

While some longed for the past, many more embraced the present. One trustee whose term was up in 1970 "only regret[s] that I am retiring in such an exciting period of challenge and of change." Another applauded the social progress and campus diversity that was spurred in part by Brown's student protests in 1968. A 1942 graduate summed it up when he said, "I . . . sincerely wish the members of the Corporation the best of luck in the handling of the problems of the '70s."

The stories of similar journeys experienced decades apart reveal hidden bonds of the Brown community. One alum expressed incredulity at his "unlikely" status as a trustee, his ability to attend Brown made possible through the financial scaffolding of an NROTC scholarship and work as a dormitory proctor and waiter throughout school—in 1946. More recent Corporation members who had been first-generation and low-income students as Brown undergraduates conveyed similar sentiments in their letters of resignation, decades later.

Brown shaped people in essential ways through searing educational and social encounters. The authors recalled significant milestones such as the launch of Brown's famed New Curriculum; the merger of The Women's College, Pembroke, with The College; the establishment of the medical school. Few wanted to leave when their time was up. I read the words "bittersweet" and "regretfully" countless times.

To be sure, not every letter is sentimental. Upon departure, many took the opportunity to freely dispense advice. In 1990, one trustee acknowledged that "some very serious choices must be made . . . to prevent Brown from sliding . . . from excellence to mediocrity." John Brown sounded a note of similar caution two hundred years earlier:

> The great Revolutionary War, in which we obtained our Independence, was a great Stagnation to our Institution . . . this circumstance [is] certainly sufficient motive . . . to step Forward and promote the College under your directions;

More than five years and five hundred letters after the idea first dawned on me, the truly challenging part began. How to choose? Almost all the letters were worthy in some way, whether wise, witty, or heartfelt. I needed help.

I called Logan Powell, Associate Provost for Enrollment and Dean of Undergraduate Admission, for guidance. Every year, his department sets the standard for how to build a real-life community out of thousands of deserving applicants. I thought some parallels could apply. Though crazed by the demands of his job in the midst of pandemic aftershocks, Logan gave me generous time and advice. I came away from our conversations with newfound clarity.

With the help of the University, I would put together a readers group, trustees and fellows who would bring different perspectives to the process. We divided up the letters so that each would be assessed by at least two unique readers. The goal was to balance my opinion as an individual with collective rigor.

I created a rubric to assist the group in its decision-making. One aspect was that the letters should help decode the Corporation experience and paint a more human portrait of this seemingly impenetrable body. For highest consideration, the letters had to be profound human snapshots. Individually, each needed to touch on a specific dynamic of the school's academic, social, cultural, or political transformations. The readers' commitment to the process and their variety of viewpoints materially shaped the book.

The letter that inspired me nearly ten years ago is included. I won't call it out here because I expect that you might find one letter or another that changes *your* perspective, perhaps because it is so very different from your own. Another might resonate precisely because its frame of reference mirrors yours. Maybe a couple will make you laugh.

The pages that follow depict the evolution of Brown's enduring traditions and help reframe perspectives on the sorts of social issues with which the University still grapples. I'm hopeful that these letters offer a glimpse of how the members of the Corporation have tried to uphold Brown's guiding principle for themselves and for future generations as we seek to lead "lives of usefulness and reputation."

The ultimate power of the collection comes from recognizing that we cannot know each other's stories until we take the time to listen.

Lauren Zalaznick
English, 1984
Trustee, 2011 – 2017

Commencement on the College Green, 1954

Foreword

BY RUTH BURT EKSTROM

"IT IS ALWAYS AN Old Brown, and it is always a New Brown," said Charles Evans Hughes, class of 1881 and Corporation fellow, sharing his observations as a loyal alumnus. The letters in this volume from former Corporation members reflect ideas and decisions that embody the importance of Brown's traditions and also its necessary progress. Each member of the Corporation brings their own unique background, skills, and knowledge and applies them to the challenges they face during their years as active members. All affirm the goal of providing students with an environment that will prepare them to lead lives of "usefulness and reputation."

The composition of the Corporation has evolved since the founding of the University, and the letters reflect this. Originally all Corporation members were appointed for life. Today there are term limits. Originally all Corporation members were white, male, and Christian (mostly Baptist), and most were wealthy. Today the Corporation has women and individuals from a variety of racial, ethnic, and religious backgrounds, bringing a wider perspective and broader set of experiences to their work.

My story is an example of this. I was a first-generation college student with a high school education more limited than most of my Brown classmates. My years at Brown transformed my life. After my graduation in 1953, I wanted to show my appreciation to the University, so I volunteered to do fundraising for my class. This led to my becoming class agent representative on the Board of the Pembroke College Alumnae Association. There I was inspired by its president, Elizabeth Goodale Kenyon, class of 1939, who was working to have women become elected alumnae trustees. This came to pass when she herself became the first, in 1965. I continued on the Pembroke Alumnae Association Board until the time of the Brown-Pembroke merger in 1971. I thought my work for Brown had ended.

So I was surprised one spring evening in 1972 to receive a phone call from Brown President Donald Hornig, who told me that I had been nominated to become a term trustee. He wanted to know if I would accept the position, and I said yes.

That fall I traveled to Brown and was sworn in as a Corporation member. Chancellor Charles Tillinghast met with some of the new trustees (I was the only woman) to explain what was expected of us. He talked about President Wriston, who had said that the qualities he looked for in Corporation members were "work, wealth, and wisdom" but that he would settle for any two of those three. I didn't have wealth, but I was eager to work hard and to share my knowledge about academic programs that I had from doing education policy research.

My term as a trustee ended in June 1977, but the Corporation office quickly contacted me to let me know that I had been elected to the Board of Fellows. Subsequently, President Swearer said that he wanted me to be the Secretary of the Corporation. This would be the first time that a woman served as a Corporation officer. I felt it was important for the Corporation members to see a woman sitting with the President and the Chancellor at the table in front of them, helping them preside over the meeting.

As Secretary, to be honest, I don't recall much about any individual letter that I read, but I do recall being somewhat nervous that I never had a chance to review the letters in advance and had to read them aloud in front of fifty-three other members of the Corporation with no practice! My eleven-year term as fellow ended in June 1988. I read my own letter aloud then. On July 1, I became a part of the group of Brown's emeriti Corporation members.

Almost seventy-five years after I first arrived on campus, I see the many ways that the "New Brown" is still evolving but coexists successfully with the best of the "Old Brown." The letters that follow help us see how that course has been charted through the service of the fellows and trustees of the Corporation.

Ruth Burt Ekstrom
Psychology, 1953
Honorary Doctor of Laws, 1988
Secretary, 1982 – 1988
Trustee, 1972 – 1977
Fellow, 1977 – 1988

BROWN UNIVERSITY
OFFICERS OF THE CORPORATION

Corporation members usually address their letters of resignation to the Corporation Secretary. On occasion, however, members also address their letters to, or make frequent mention of, Brown's Presidents, Chancellors, and others who play an indispensable role in the life of the University. The terms of the officers, which represent the trustees' and fellows' years of service and their graduation years, are 1764 – 1803 and 1905 – 2023.

Many of the letters from every era have not yet been found. We continue to search for them.

Presidents

James Manning	1765 – 1791
Jonathan Maxcy	1797 – 1802
Asa Messer	1803 – 1826
——	
William Herbert Perry Faunce	1899 – 1929
Clarence Augustus Barbour	1929 – 1937
Henry Merritt Wriston	1937 – 1955
Barnaby Conrad Keeney	1955 – 1966
Ray Lorenzo Heffner	1966 – 1969
Donald Frederick Hornig	1970 – 1976
Howard Robert Swearer	1977 – 1988
Vartan Gregorian	1989 – 1997
E. Gordon Gee	1998 – 2000
Sheila E. Blumstein	2000 – 2001 [acting]
Ruth J. Simmons	2001 – 2012
Christina H. Paxson	2012 –

Chancellors of the University

Stephen Hopkins	1764 – 1785
Jabez Bowen	1785 – 1815
——	
William Goddard	1888 – 1907
Arnold Buffum Chace	1907 – 1932
Henry D. Sharpe	1932 – 1952
Harold Brooks Tanner	1952 – 1964
Hugh Stanford McLeod	1964 – 1968
Charles Carpenter Tillinghast, Jr.	1968 – 1979
Richard Salomon	1979 – 1988
Alva O. Way	1988 – 1997
Artemis A. W. Joukowsky, Jr.	1997 – 1998
Stephen Robert	1998 – 2007
Thomas J. Tisch	2007 – 2016
Samuel M. Mencoff	2016 – 2024

Vice Chancellors of the University

Donald G. Millar	1964 – 1968
Alfred H. Joslin	1968 – 1969
Foster B. Davis, Jr.	1969 – 1979
Thomas J. Watson, Jr.	1979 – 1985
Henry D. Sharpe, Jr.	1985 – 1988
Artemis A.W. Joukowsky, Jr.	1988 – 1997
Stephen Robert	1997 – 1998
Marie J. Langlois	1998 – 2007
Jerome C. Vascellaro	2007 – 2016
Alison S. Ressler	2016 – 2022
Pamela R. Reeves	2022 – 2025

Secretaries of the Corporation

Thomas Eyres	1764 – 1776
Thomas Arnold	1776 – 1780
David Howell	1780 – 1806

———

Thomas Davis Anderson	1890 – 1924
Hermon Carey Bumpus	1924 – 1937
Albert Lyon Scott	1937 – 1945
Fred Bartlett Perkins	1945 – 1963
John Nicholas Brown	1963 – 1972
Alfred Hahn Joslin	1972 – 1982
Ruth Burt Ekstrom	1982 – 1988
Henry D. Sharpe, Jr.	1988 – 1998
Wendy J. Strothman	1998 – 2008
Donald C. Hood	2008 – 2017
Richard A. Friedman	2017 – 2026

Treasurers

John Tillinghast	1764 – 1767
Job Bennett	1767 – 1775
John Brown	1775 – 1796
Nicholas Brown	1796 – 1825

––––

Cornelius Sowle Sweetland	1900 – 1923
Frank Willington Matteson	1923 – 1933
Harold Crins Field	1934 – 1947
George Burton Hibbert	1947 – 1950
Gordon Lancaster Parker	1950 – 1965
Patrick James James	1965 – 1970
Joseph William Ress	1970 – 1979
Andrew Martin Hunt	1979 – 1988
Marie J. Langlois	1988 – 1992
Martha Clark Goss	1992 – 1998
Matthew J. Mallow	1998 – 2008
Alison S. Ressler	2008 – 2016
Theresia Gouw	2016 – 2025

Editor's note: Some of the letters in this book have been lightly edited for space, to correct typographical errors, or to redact personal information. Original spelling and grammar have been preserved in the late-eighteenth- and early-nineteenth-century letters. These letters are addressed to the Corporation of Rhode Island College, which was renamed Brown University in 1804.

The Letters

University Hall, 1907

An Inefficient Majesty

The broad, slow process of achieving consensus on
issues and actions on the campus lumbers along toward
rightness and fitness with a kind of inefficient majesty.

—VINCENT J. BUONANNO

———

Italian, 1966
Trustee, 1985 – 1991, 1998 – 2004

May 23, 2019
Secretary Richard Friedman
Brown University Corporation
1 Prospect Street
Providence, RI 02912

Dear Rich,

My great-grandfather, Alexander Hardiman, was a gravedigger. Family lore has it that Alexander, the son of slaves, walked the streets of the Arkansas town in which he lived asking, "Who will build *my* grave?" Now, there was a practical dimension to this inquiry, as he was the only gravedigger in town. But there was more than just that. Alexander's question was not merely about the practicalities of death. Rather, it went to his life as a poor, black man in the Jim Crow South. What legacy could he leave? What lasting contribution could he hope to make?

If someone had told me thirty years ago, as I prepared to graduate from Brown University, that this Corporation would one day help me find my own answers to these questions, I probably would have laughed. To the extent I thought of this body at all, it was as an exclusive, predominantly white and male institution that would never find its way to incorporate someone like me, an African American woman, into in its ranks. It never occurred to me that it would one day be an avenue for me to give back, to begin to repay, if only in small ways, the many sacrifices that made it possible for me and others like me to come to Brown in the first place.

Nineteen of the last thirty years are ones that I have spent directly and happily engaged with the Brown University Corporation. After two years serving as a non-Corporation member of the predecessor to the Campus Life Committee, I was invited to join the Board of Trustees and, seven years later, to become a member of the Board of Fellows. During my tenure on the Corporation, I have had a front row seat to the amazing change and development that the University has undergone in recent years. I am fortunate to have served under three different presidents, Sheila Blumstein; Ruth Simmons, the first African American woman to serve as an Ivy president; and Christina Paxson, the current and extremely capable steward of our beloved university. I have worked with three chancellors, Steve Robert, Tom Tisch, and Sam Mencoff. Additionally, I have witnessed the launch of two major academic initiatives—Boldly Brown and Building on Distinction—and at least as many major funding campaigns. Finally, I have seen our endowment grow in a way that has made need-blind admissions and a promise of no loans a reality at Brown.

In many ways, I "became" myself during this period. My service on the Corporation corresponded with a legal career that began with civil rights work and led to a position in academia addressing the same concerns. It also marked the start of a family life that sustains me in so many ways. Following my "engagement" as a trustee, I became engaged to and then married to my beloved partner, Bill Crawley. I also became the mother of our two wonderful children, Caleb and Aidan.

I could not be more grateful for the many gifts that service on the Corporation these many years has provided me. In addition to deep friendships that I cherish, I am grateful for what membership on the Corporation has taught me about giving and leadership in particular. With respect to the former, I learned what my six-year-old son would describe as the "everyone is big enough" approach. Under this way of thinking, while big gifts of money or even time are certainly welcome, they are not required. Instead, priority is placed on each person doing what they can, when they can. This tenet recognizes the diverse backgrounds and talents of those in the Brown community and creates opportunities for everyone to make a difference in a way that I appreciate so very much.

On leadership, there is not enough time or ink for me to address all that I have learned about that subject and institutional change these many years. All I will say here is that I am grateful to have been given so many opportunities to serve and hope that I managed to make a difference here and there. Highlights for me were collaborating on campus life issues with my dear friend Laura Geller, often early in the morning, and addressing matters of governance. It was my honor to work with Diana Wells, Craig Barton, Ralph Rosenburg, and Laura on a process for officer transition that led to the selection of our current chancellor, as well as our treasurer and secretary. It also meant a great deal for me to work with that same group, as well as Joan Sorensen and the indefatigable Jerome Vascellaro, on governance reforms that are already paying dividends, both in terms of how we approach and feel about the work we do together as a body. Importantly, none of what we accomplished together could have been achieved without the much appreciated support and insight provided by Russell Carey, Catherine Pincince, and Amalia Davis.

I often wonder what great-grandfather Alexander would say if he were alive today. I hope that he would be happy with what I and others in my family have been able to achieve because of his sacrifices. Part of me knows, however, that he would likely also urge us to push harder, to do more for more people. So, I will close this letter with a similar exhortation. We have achieved so much at Brown. Yet, we have so much more to do, for our students, especially those from underrepresented groups; the community in which we sit; and the world of which we are a part. Be boldly Brown! The need for such action has never been greater.

Ever true,

Robin A. Lenhardt
English, 1989
Trustee, 2000 – 2006
Fellow, 2008 – 2019

American Baptist Convention

Office of the General Secretary

VALLEY FORGE, PENNSYLVANIA 19481

Edwin H. Tuller, General Secretary • Frank E. Johnston, W. Hubert Porter, Associate General Secretaries

September 17, 1969

Mr. John Nicholas Brown
Secretary, Brown University
Providence, Rhode Island 02912

Dear Mr. Brown:

In accordance with established procedure with which I agree fully I hereby tender my resignation as a Trustee of Brown University after having completed the term for which I was elected. Unfortunately, a previous assignment in St. Louis, which I cannot change, makes it impossible for me to attend the last meeting of the Corporation during my term of office. I will ask you, therefore, to present my resignation at that time in my absence.

Over two hundred years ago Brown University was founded by Baptist people who sought to establish a college dedicated to free academic inquiry and to establishing the highest standards of education available for young men. Over the centuries they have continued their interest and I trust that Baptist people will always remember with deep appreciation the many contributions of that infant college now grown to full maturity as one of the outstanding educational institutions in the country. While Brown is no longer officially related to the American Baptist Convention, I still feel a sense of pride in having been able to be for a short period of time a kind of link between the Baptist people and this great university. I trust that the future will not completely forget the historic roots of Brown and that the spiritual foundations of the institution might continue to exist and to guide the University as it seeks to discharge its obligations both to the succeeding generations and to the public at large. You will always have my interest and support and Brown will continue to be an important part of my life. Thank you for the privilege of serving as a Trustee.

Cordially,

Edwin H. Tuller

Edwin H. Tuller
General Secretary

EHT:kh

Telephones (area code 215): Dr. Tuller 768-2274, Dr. Johnston 768-2293, Dr. Porter 768-2277

Edwin H. Tuller

Economics, 1935

Honorary Doctor of Divinity, 1956

Trustee, 1962 – 1969

May 8, 2015

Dear Don,

In accordance with the terms of my election, I respectfully resign as a trustee of Brown University effective June 30, 2015.

One of my favorite quotes about Brown is Jeffrey Eugenides's description of the Brown seal in the opening pages of *The Marriage Plot*. He describes Brown's sun as having a "sagacious face," and as he talks about the Brown seal in comparison to an actual Providence sunrise on Commencement, he notes "this sun—the one over Providence—was doing the metaphorical sun one better, because the founders of the University, in their Baptist pessimism, had chosen to depict the light of knowledge enshrouded by clouds, indicating that ignorance had not yet been dispelled from the human realm, whereas the actual sun was just now fighting its way through cloud cover, sending down splintered beams of light and giving hope to the squadrons of parents, who'd been soaked and frozen all weekend, that the unseasonable weather might not ruin the day's festivities."

To me, the Corporation is a personification of these two suns, and I feel so fortunate to have had the honor to serve Brown as a young alumna trustee for the last three years. While we haven't yet figured out how to ensure that graduation happens rain-free, we are using our sagacious faces—our wisdom and our knowledge—to rise above the clouds and take actions that, in true Brown and Rhode Island spirit, increase hope. And it's been a delight to get to see your sunny faces in rainy Octobers, snowy Februarys, and rainy Mays!

I look forward to following how the Brunonian sun continues to beat through the clouds and continuing to engage with and support Brown in the years to come.

Alison Cohen

———

Alison K. Cohen
Community Health and Education Studies, 2009
Trustee, 2012 – 2015

Elie Hirschfeld

May 11, 1999

The Corporation
Brown University
Providence, Rhode Island 02912

Dear Friends of Brown:

As if it were only yesterday, I recall a moment in time some 30 years ago when I was a student at Brown. I heard there was a Corporation Room at University Hall and I wondered what that room must be like. I set out, apprehensively, to see this formidable place. I sneaked up the stairs and I remember peeking in.

I imagined that here must sit omniscient statesmen and other supreme all-knowing people divinely determining Brown's fate. It turns out that my premonition was right.

I will miss all of you all-knowing friends of Brown.

Here is my resignation from the Corporation but, like others before me, I will never resign from my love and affection for all of you and for Brown. I am here for good.

Sincerely,

Elie Hirschfeld
Class of 1971

Elie Hirschfeld

Economics and Mathematics, 1971

Trustee, 1992 – 1999

The Corporation meets on the third floor of
University Hall, Brown's oldest edifice erected in
1770, in the eponymously named Corporation Room.

May 27, 2022

Dear Rich:

It was a little more than 20 years ago that Steve Robert asked me if l would join the Brown Corporation as a Trustee.

I said yes, of course, excited by the possibilities. Yet a question kept coming back to me as I am sure it did for so many others: How could a 54-person governing body for a university actually work?

I am happy to say that after these two decades I have the answer: It works magnificently.

It turns out that there is great genius in our Charter from 1764.

The size of 54, which seems unwieldy from the outside, is big enough to reflect the breadth of our community without being a fractured or sectarian body. We're bigger than a clique, yet smaller than the Congress. We aren't a representative body, but our cohesion is critical and consequential to Brown's success. One voice, one observation can move the whole of us. And, while we are never supposed to be "management," the breadth of our skills and backgrounds is a trusted resource for a whole array of tricky moments and issues.

Our size offers a wide diversity of age and perspectives on the world and on Brown. I have been lucky to serve with Trustees and Fellows whose vivid recollections of personalities, events and institutional decisions could take me back to the Brown of the 1950s under President Henry Merritt Wriston, allowing that pivotal decade to come alive with great texture, clarity and relevance.

Remarkably, Steve Robert, who brought me onto the Corporation in 2002, had been a member of the Corporation since 1984, when there were seven members of the Corporation from Classes of the 1930s and six Emeriti members with graduating classes of now a hundred or more years ago. It is almost as if, by being on the Corporation and among the Emeriti, with one degree of separation one can feel the long arc of the generations, the temporal equivalent of seeing the curvature of the Earth, something not apparent when one stands alone at the seashore.

These are but a few of the observations which, with the perspective of 20 years, have helped me to appreciate the genius in our Charter.

The fact is that the Brown Corporation is the deep keel of the University, built with balance and structured to take the long view, and one never stuck in the present. If the 50 states are America's laboratories of democracy, our universities are our laboratories of community—and ones animated by the optimism of youth, the power of learning and the advancement of knowledge. The possibilities of the future are always present. This optimism that is at our core is one that has refreshed itself for centuries. What a beautiful thing.

Brown—given our Charter, campus, curriculum, structure, scale, and diversity—is a marvelous canvas. Somehow, at Brown, goodness is as important as greatness, an idea constantly refreshed by the purposeful character of our work together.

In fact, the meshing of goodness and greatness—mixing humility and openness with the absolute highest of aspirations and achievement—is something that is elemental to Brown; it is present in our Charter, in so many aspects of the University, in our leadership and in the Corporation. This is something that is so natural to Brown, so much a part of our history and ethos, and it is among the reasons that our work together is so satisfying.

There is also a deep kindness in our group that is a corporation. It is as if there is a pact that into this place and into this room, we bring our best selves. That is something I've always felt myself and about everyone in this room.

I have been lucky to see the consequence that Brown has enjoyed by virtue of the great leadership over these past 20 years.

> Chris—who is a member of this body—and similarly Ruth before her AND the Senior Administration, so many members of whom are with us today, have been so critical to our—and Brown's—success.

> Amalia, Catherine and Russell, who are our support, have with efficiency and good cheer kept us organized, focused and on schedule. Remarkably, each has served for the full duration of the terms of just about every person in this room.

I've been lucky to see Brown for close to 50 years—and to see the University from a variety of perspectives. One thing is clear: Brown's uniqueness and specialness have deep roots. Seeing Brown through the shared lens of the Corporation is a sublime and special privilege and one whose camaraderie has spawned so many lasting friendships for me and, happily, for Alice. For this past year, I have taken pleasure in sitting back a little and relishing how we function—how YOU function—and, in leaving on June 30th, I have the deep satisfaction of knowing that our beloved Brown is in your hands.

Ever true,

Thomas Jonah Tisch

———

Thomas J. Tisch
Religious Studies, 1976
Honorary Doctor of Humane Letters, 2022
Chancellor, 2007 – 2016
Trustee, 2002 – 2016
Fellow, 2017 – 2022

> "You have convinced me, at least momentarily,
> that resignation is a privilege."

THOMAS B. APPLEGET
ROUND HILL ROAD
GREENWICH, CONNECTICUT

May 15, 1963.

Dear Fred,

your letters of re-
minders to Term Trustees, like
all your actions, are master-
pieces of tact. you have
convinced me, at least mo-
mentarily, that resignation
is a privilege.

As a matter of fact,
I think it is time that
this very venerable institution
and this slightly venerable
trustee should be relieved
of their official responsibilities,
each to the other. We
both deserve a vacation.
The statistics of our of-
ficial relationships support
this decision.

I find that during
the forty-six years since

from the Univer-
... officially
... a total of
... eighteen years
... and twenty-three
... and, finally
... my first
... Corporation
... three years
... as assistant
...
... particularly
... privilege
... final term
... was some
... I felt that
... and grace-
... my
...
... forward to
... as a
... with no
obligations save those im-
posed by loyalty and
affection.

Sincerely

Thomas B. Appleget.

Thomas B. Appleget
Bachelor of Philosophy, 1917
Honorary Doctor of Laws, 1967
Trustee, 1928 – 1934, 1935 – 1949, 1960 – 1963

May 15, 2009

Mr. Donald Hood

Secretary, Brown Corporation

Brown University

Box 1887

Providence, RI 02912

Re: Letter of Resignation

Dear Don,

When I was asked to join the Board of Trustees, I wasn't sure they really wanted me if they knew I was one of those kids outside picketing the Corporation—the issue at that time was divestiture of assets from South Africa due to apartheid. Back then, we figured the Board was just a group of white collar businessmen who were out of touch with what was going on. I had no idea that I would someday become one of "them." Fortunately, my youthful perceptions couldn't have been further from the truth. During my time on the Board, it's become clear that Corporation members are engaged, dedicated, and genuine in terms of their love and commitment to Brown.

Having had the privilege of serving on the board for quite some time now, I've listened to a number of these letters. They range from the heartfelt bittersweet emotions to being entertaining and funny. Marty Granoff's comedic style was a classic! While I certainly feel that range of emotions, in the end, I feel so blessed to have had this opportunity to serve the Brown that I've come to know and love. The teamwork and relationships that have been developed with colleagues and staff have been extremely rewarding and inspirational.

It's rare to have an opportunity to work with brilliant people who share a passion, and be in a position to contribute time and resources to make meaningful impacts on Brown for decades to come. In this challenging environment we're facing, it's comforting to know that our beloved Brown is in great hands and will continue to higher levels of success.

Again, I thank God for the opportunity to serve and enjoy such a gratifying experience.

Ever True,

Steven R. Jordan

Engineering, 1982

Honorary Doctor of Humane Letters, 2021

Trustee, 1993 – 1997

Fellow, 1998 – 2009

Corporation members Gordon E. Cadwgan 1936, Marvyn Carton 1938, and Foster
Davis 1939 (left to right) are confronted by student protestors, February 1986

Marvyn Carton
711 Fifth Avenue
New York

April 14, 1987

Mrs. Ruth B. Ekstrom
Secretary of the Corporation
Brown University
Providence, R.I. 02912

Dear Ruth:

The "time" has [finally] arrived, which unhappy date I've
anguished over since I felt I could never create as witty, clever,
or amusing a letter of resignation as any of those read during
the past six years. The trauma of waiting is now over and I'm
glad; I resign.

Notwithstanding the foregoing, I have always felt honored
and privileged having been a member of this distinguished group
and also because of the warm affection I've felt for this institution
since I became a freshman in 1934. This place, because of reasons
peculiar to myself, became a home to me when I was a student.

My contribution to the deliberations of this body I fear
were small; this, because most of my working life has been spent
in a business where definitive decisions are very frequently made,
either "yes or no," - never "maybe". The careful consideration given
to some matters by this august body was a revelation to me. As a
result of all this attention to minute detail, which I at first
found frustrating, I eventually realized that one could always find
comfort in one or more of the many views expressed and that it was
also possible to reach a conclusion which embraced "yes, no and maybe."

In closing, may I say I am grateful for this experience and
the opportunity to have met and worked with all of you.

Sincerely,

MC:rl

Marvyn Carton
Economics, 1938
Trustee, 1981 – 1987

May 19, 2017

Dear Chris,

Don is probably saying that he doesn't remember writing this letter. Actually, this is understandable as his Superego is speaking and is typically in charge of such things—very pushy this Superego. The truth is, I (his Ego) wrote this letter while the Superego was asleep. I had help, if you want to call it that, from our Id.

First, Id and I want to address the email asking for this resignation letter—an email sent to us by him as Secretary. I won't print the Id's comments in detail, but it started, and I quote, "Who does he think he is? —Us?—This is bullshit" and it went downhill from there. I have to confess as the Ego, I thought an exception would be made for us. But, our Superego spoiled that by asking us to resign.

In any case, I am sure I am speaking for the three of us in saying it has been an incredible, and wonderful, experience. When you join a board, you join a family. And, some families, and some boards, are dysfunctional. This group, however, has been fantastic. It has been amazing to the Id and me to see how Corporation members suppress their egos and ids, and focused on our common goal—Brown. (Actually, at this point Id wanted to mention one or two exceptions a few years back, but I knew the Superego would not approve.) Of course, the focus on purpose, and not the individual, has been due, in no small part, to Ruth and Chris, the two greatest academic leaders the three of us have seen in our over 50 years in the academy.

In closing, the three of us thank them and all of you. We will miss you.

Sincerely,

Don, Don & Don
PS. Written by Don's Ego with interference from his Id.

———

Donald C. Hood
Master of Science, Psychology, 1968
Doctor of Philosophy, Psychology, 1970
Honorary Doctor of Humane Letters, 2017
Secretary, 2008 – 2017
Fellow, 2001 – 2017

SHUKUTOKU UNIVERSITY
THE COLLEGE OF CROSS-CULTURAL COMMUNICATION AND BUSINESS

Dean of the College
Noritake   Kobayashi

May 20, 1997

Mr. Henry D. Sharpe Jr.
Secretary
Brown University
Providence
Rhode Island 02912
U. S. A.

Dear Mr. Sharpe:

It was in the early summer of 1991 that I took an oath of loyalty to Brown University and was initiated officially as a trustee by Former Chancellor Alva Way to this Corporation Meeting.   I felt I was greatly honored and I was very proud of the nomination because Brown is one of the Universities I most admired.   My son graduated from this University in 1985 and I was the first member of the Corporation without U. S. citizenship.

Looking back on my term as a trustee, I feel it has been a great new life and experience.

I was very much impressed by the loyalty and devotion of the members of the Corporation, faculty, alumni and Parents' Council to the University.   Their untiring effort has resulted in the success of the greatest fundraising campaign ever engaged by Brown under the outstanding leadership of President Vartan Gregorian.

In the beginning, I was somewhat surprised to witness the free exchange of ideas in the Corporation Meetings.   It was much freer than I normally expect in a meeting of a similar nature in my country.   Everyone seemed to have a principle for which he stood and everyone had a broad mind when listening to others who might not share the same principle, for example, their treatment of minority and gender problems.   The outcome of the discussion was always very constructive.   As I continued to attend the meetings over the years, I felt that I learned about the essence of freedom of speech, which is a strong pillar of democracy, and the importance of openness.

I am grateful to the Corporation and the University for all the heart-warming friendship which was extended to me.

Whenever I came to Providence after a long air-trip from Tokyo, I had a home to stay at, the beautiful historic residence of Art and Martha Joukowsky. I had shared many happy occasions with members of the Corporation at the committee meetings, Presidential lunches, receptions, forums, pop concerts in the yard and the graduation processions up and down the hill. These dear memories and friendships will remain in my mind for a long time to come.

Now, I am leaving the Corporation as a trustee. However, the work which I started a few years ago, Brown University's Centennial Fundraising Campaign in Japan, is still continuing in Tokyo. This is a very important project because I believe strongly that the exchange of educational opportunities on a grass-roots level, the undergraduate level, in addition to those of the higher professional schools, is essential for the better understanding of the peoples and societies belonging to two great nations of the world, the United States and Japan.

I should like to repeat once again my sincere thanks to you and the members of the Corporation for all the kind friendships and great experiences which I have enjoyed in the past six years. I very much hope that you and the Corporation will continue to develop and prosper into the forthcoming New Great Century.

Sincerely yours,

Noritake Kobayashi
Professor Emeritus, Keio University
Dean, the College of Cross-Cultural
Communication and Business,
Shukutoku University

Noritake Kobayashi
Parent, 1985
Trustee, 1991 – 1997

McLeod Associates, Inc.

MANAGEMENT INFORMATION SYSTEMS CONSULTANTS

May 16, 2007

Ms. Wendy Strothman
Secretary
Office of the Corporation
Brown University
P. O. Box 1887
Providence, RI   02912

Dear Wendy,

I resign! [*Stage Pause*]

On second thought, that statement of resignation is much too short. So, stay tuned for the longer version....

Over the past six years, I have listened to numerous resignation letters written by members of this august Corporation. Now, alas, the time has come for me to write mine. A six-year term seemed like such a long time at the beginning, but it passed all too quickly.

When I arrived in Providence for the first time in September of 1964, little did I think that I would become so attached to this university. In fact, when I graduated four years later (39 years ago now), I had no intention of <u>ever</u> returning to Providence much less to Brown, but "things happened" and I, in my youthful folly, was proven wrong.

In 1970, I returned to Providence to take courses in Applied Math and Computer Science, after having been hired by IBM in New York City. The very next year, in 1971, Brown's Manning Chapel became the site of my wedding. I left Providence again, well assured that there was certainly no need at all for me to ever return. Indeed, I stayed away for 8 years, until a "reach-out" from Brown lured me back into the fold. Since that time, my involvement with and love for Brown and my Brown family have grown immeasurably.

Please forgive a tear or two from me as I'm forced to listen to my own words. After all, I was the kid who cried when my father traded in an old car for a new one. Of course, this is not to say that leaving the status of "current trustee" is analogous to giving up an old car. It's just acknowledging that "parting can be such sweet sorrow". In actuality, I'm graduating to the rank of "emerita" in good company as evidenced by all of us who have letters that will be read today. I promise to wear that badge with honor. So a celebration is in order instead of tears.

Bernicestine McLeod Bailey

Economics, 1968

Honorary Doctor of Humane Letters, 2023

Trustee, 2001 – 2007

After being involved with Brown in so many ways over the years, I do say that it was a truly special experience for me to be a member of this Corporation during this particular time and space. We as a university have grown so very much over the past six years on many levels. However, there is certainly work for me to do still on my Brown journey. Ending my term as a "current trustee" is by no means the culmination of my service to Brown. I just have greater insight now as to how I can really be of service and am much more inspired. So, although I've been promoted to emerita, I don't intend to "sit on a beach" (well, that is, maybe I shall next week but for no longer than a week). I've heeded the words of our president delivered in a recent speech (loosely paraphrased) that "if you aren't feeling pain, you have not served enough".

Diversity and all that it encompasses is so near and dear to me. I am pleased with the progress we have made here especially when I look back over the forty-three years since I first arrived on campus. However, there is still much to be done and I look forward to continuing in that arena in whatever capacity.

Be well! May the force be with you!

Sincerely,

Bernicestine McLeod Bailey

University Hall Takeover, 1992

"Having been a member of this Corporation
above thirty years, in which it has advanced
from Small beginings to high respectability
among mankind . . . I request liberty
to resign my place in your Corporation; praying
that the Divine blessing may ever attend
this Seminary of learning for the good of
mankind to the latest generation."

———

Reverend Isaac Backus
Honorary Master of Arts, 1797
Trustee, 1765 – 1799

To the Corporation of Rhode Island College.

Reverend and Honored Gentlemen.

Having been a member of this Corporation above thirty years, in which it has advanced from small beginings to high respectability among mankind, and as my age & infirmities are such as to make it very difficult to attend your meetings any longer, I request liberty to resign my place in your Corporation; praying that the Divine blessing may ever attend this Seminary of learning for the good of mankind to the latest generation.

I remain your hearty friend and servant,

Isaac Backus.

Middleborough,
Sept. 2. 1799.

2. 1799.

.41.
37.

7.
3.

4

42

7. 8. 1/3
3. 37. 1/3
_____
3. 75

The Brown Ballroom Dancing
Club dances on the College
Green, February 1990

What Makes Brown, "Brown"

Brown makes you feel like you can do anything, and gives you the strength of character and work ethic to see your passions through. Brown teaches creativity, teamwork, and persistence—the tools to make dreams a reality. I think this is what makes our school special.

—SRIHARI S. NAIDU

———

Neuroscience, 1993
Doctor of Medicine, 1997
Trustee, 2013 – 2019

June 1, 1977

Dear Judge Joslin:

When I was nominated to become a member of the Corporation of Brown University I agreed to resign at the end of my term. I made that agreement without any mental reservation. Now, both because I have enjoyed the experience so much, and because I have recently passed a bar examination, I have begun to wonder whether my promise to resign is legally enforceable.

It is only because of my hesitation to overburden the courts, and the University, with even more litigation that I have refrained from filing suit.

When I was a student at Brown a fair amount of my time was involved in student government affairs and particularly in curricular reform. I can remember the many hours that I spent talking to members of the Student Life Committee. I can also remember my extraordinary lack of knowledge about the Corporation, and my concern about the fate of proposals for change which had to be considered by this "unrepresentative" group. Walt Kelly was right, however—we have found the enemy, and it is us.

It has been a great privilege to serve on the Corporation. The men and women who served with me have given of themselves in many ways. I have learned enormously from them and count them as my friends.

But I should not let my last formal statement be all sweetness and light. The Corporation has begun—but has only begun—to play the role which I believe it must. It should not involve itself in the day-to-day management of the University. But it should constantly question the administration, playing the role of informed and loving observer. It should devise, and constantly refine, mechanisms such as the Student Life Committee, which I was lucky enough to join, to receive input from the major constituencies of the University. It must be provided access to information before its meetings. The meetings should be scheduled so as to increase productive discussions rather than being used for the reading of reports which could be mailed out and summarized during our limited time together.

I have only two regrets. One is the constant regret of not having worked harder and given more. The other is that my term is over. I hope that I can continue to assist the University and that you and the Corporation will not hesitate to call on me. Please express my thanks to all the members of the Corporation who have made this experience such a memorable one for me. And please also extend my thanks to the members of the University Hall staff whose time and effort have held us together.

Very truly yours,

Elliot E. Maxwell

Elliot E. Maxwell
American Civilization, 1968
Honorary Doctor of Humane Letters, 1994
Trustee, 1972 – 1977

Editor's Note: Undergraduate students Elliot Maxwell 1968 and Ira Magaziner 1969 led a campus-wide movement to examine all aspects of learning and teaching at Brown. The subsequent reforms were adapted in May 1969. Those educational principles became the backbone of Brown's Open Curriculum, which, with very little modification, is still the model in use today, notably unique to Brown.

May 10, 2002

Wendy J. Strothman Secretary of the Corporation
Box 1887
Brown University Providence, RI 02912

Dear Wendy,

After an exciting and challenging term as trustee, it is indeed a difficult duty for me to write this letter of resignation from the Corporation of Brown University. The last six years have been a whirlwind of activity dealing with important issues affecting my alma mater. Not surprisingly, my efforts for Brown in this position were accompanied by a full range of human emotion: some exciting, some frustrating, some tiring, some inspiring, some educational, some insightful, most enjoyable, and all accompanied by enthusiasm and gusto. Whatever I have done for Brown, my thoughts always seem to circle back to the students, Brown's young adult students, who are our yearly legacy to the future of our country.

My trustee journey was much like a well lived life—initially learning, then more understanding, and then doing—all in the context of an institution with a noble purpose that continues to evolve and grow and always striving to improve. What I have loved about Brown, which I have seen from the trustee viewpoint, is the desire of the place to continually get better, and to encourage alumni, parents, friends and others to participate in that betterment, to make a difference at Brown. I see in Brown a willingness to take risks and to see the future with different eyes and perhaps take a different path. This is remarkable from an institution that is well into its third century. I feel proud to have been part of decisions of the Corporation that will affect our beloved institution far into the future; I am delighted to have exposed the strength of Brown's Engineering Division to the broader Brown community and helped advance that academic department's cause for technology students in the years to come; and I am gratified to have encouraged other alumni and non alumni to become interested in Brown's mission.

It's been a great six years and I wish all new trustees who follow good luck and Godspeed as they grapple with their own issues and decisions.

Very truly yours,

Thomas W. Berry, '69

———

Thomas W. Berry
Engineering, 1969
Trustee, 1996 – 2002, 2004 – 2010

May 29, 2004

Ms. Wendy J. Strothman
Secretary
Brown University
Office of the Corporation
Box 1887
Providence, RI 02912

Re: <u>Letter of Resignation</u>

Dear Wendy:

In accordance with the terms of my election, please consider this letter as formal notification that I am resigning as a member of the Brown University Board of Trustees.

I am honored to have had the opportunity to serve for six years as a member of the Corporation. And I am proud to have been a steward of our mission to serve the community, the nation, and the world by educating and preparing students (in the words of our College Charter) to "discharge the offices of life with usefulness and reputation."

The last few years we witnessed a period of renewed excitement at Brown with the election of Ruth Simmons, a leader of exceptional talent, as our 18th President and the adoption of the Plan for Academic Enrichment, the blueprint for Brown's far-reaching aspirations. And it was very satisfying to observe the leadership of Chancellor Stephen Robert, who by example has taught us the wisdom of Ralph Waldo Emerson's words: "What lies behind us and what lies before us are small matters compared to what lies within us."

As you know, I grew up in Gary, Indiana. One of four children raised by a single mom. Even though I ranked first in my high school class, I was discouraged from applying to Brown. A guidance counselor insisted that the product of a poor,

2

all-black urban school would not be at home in the Ivy League. Fortunately, my years in Providence proved her wrong.

Brown opened my eyes to our kaleidoscopic world. I learned to think critically, to challenge old paradigms, to become open to new experiences while forging lifetime friendships. And, I enjoyed every moment.

Whenever I'm in Providence, I stroll along the campus greens, recalling my days as a young girl filled with dreams. I am renewed and challenged to think about who I may yet become. I meet our talented and exuberant students who volunteer how much they love Brown. I tell them I feel the same way.

The pursuit of excellence has long been a hallmark of Brown. Since our founding in 1764, Brown has endeavored to assemble promising students and distinguished faculty in a community designed to stimulate, even inspire, our members to develop their talents to the fullest. Today, I depart the Corporation confident that our great university, fortified by vigorous leadership, prudent planning and new ideas, is embarked on a course that will ensure our preeminence in the coming decades.

A popular commercial asks, "What can Brown do for you?" I can testify that our Brown offers an education that fosters inquiry, innovation and service to others.

Ever true,

Anita V. Spivey, '74

Anita V. Spivey
Political Science, 1974
Trustee, 1998 – 2004, 2007 – 2013

What Makes Brown, "Brown" | 33

. . . to sit with graduates whose services have helped chart Brown's successful contribution to the cultural world fulfills my long-lived hopes.

—HUNTER S. MARSTON

———

Bachelor of Philosophy, 1908
Honorary Doctor of Laws, 1963
Trustee, 1930 – 1936, 1957 – 1960, 1961 – 1964

May 13, 2020

Dear Rich,

It is with great sadness and hope that I submit my resignation from the Brown Corporation. How do I put into words my gratitude to a community that has changed not just my life, but that of my entire family?

The quote: "you are your ancestors' wildest dreams" immediately comes to my mind. My grandfather studied under the streetlights every night in Vietnam because his home didn't have electricity. Despite being a top student in Vietnam, my mother had to drop out of community college to raise me. The idea that within a generation, their grandson and son would be able to attend an institution like Brown, let alone serve on its board, would have been unfathomable. The Brown education and experience changed my life and is the root of my love for this institution.

As I look at my classmates, other alumni, and the current student body, I see the same love and appreciation for our university. I see it in initiatives like the Brown Promise. I see it in the protests and walk-outs organized. I see it in the *Brown Daily Herald* op-eds written. I see love in students and alumni dedicating time and energy to causes simply because they love Brown enough to believe that it can be an even better, more inclusive space. It is a love, I truly believe, that is uniquely Brown.

As I leave the Corporation, I look forward to watching the life-changing work that you all will continue to do and I'm even more excited to continue serving Brown from the outside. I am excited to continue to engage, advocate, and push for a more equitable Brown, out of hope and out of love, just like Brown taught me to and just like my ancestors would have dreamed.

Best,

Viet

———

Viet Nguyen
Education Studies, 2017
Trustee, 2018 – 2020

Elizabeth Jackson Phillips, 1945

WAYNE STATE UNIVERSITY

SCHOOL OF SOCIAL WORK   DETROIT, MICHIGAN 48202

June 1, 1978

Judge Alfred H. Joslin
Secretary of the Corporation
Brown University
Providence, R. I.

Dear Judge Joslin:

It is with regret that I tender my resignation as a trustee of the
Corporation. Where have the past five years gone? I have just begun
to make a contribution!! These and many other sentiments are crowding
through my mind as this letter is written.

As the first black woman to serve on the Board, I was singularly honored
and privileged. However, geographic distance and academic teaching
responsibilities made it less possible to participate regularly in
committee activities. Hopefully, other black women will serve on the
corporation in the future and make significant inputs.

For the past five years the experience of being an alumna, a trustee, and
a faculty person (though at another university) have combined to provide
me with a unique and enriched perspective of the critical role Brown
University has in the education and preparation of young people for solid
as well as notable social functioning in a complex society.

Now that my term is at an end, it is my determination to continue to be
involved and active with Brown and to serve in whatever capacity possible.
Only in this way is it possible to demonstrate my gratitude for what help
Brown has given me. I wish to work to help ensure that other Afro-
American students receive the unique benefits of a quality education from
our university.

Sincerely yours,

Elizabeth J. Phillips
Associate Professor

EJP:ss

Elizabeth Jackson Phillips

Sociology, 1945

Trustee, 1973 – 1978

I want to thank the Corporation for allowing me, a
non-alum, to experience the "Brown Way." I hope I
can come back in my next life as a Brown student.

—JOHN J. HANNAN

———

Parent, 2010, 2014, 2014
Trustee, 2011 – 2017

May 2017

Dear Don,

I prefer to think of this not as a letter of resignation, but as a letter of graduation, of celebration. So many of my wonderful colleagues on the Corporation have had the benefit of a four-year Brown education. I, however, have had a far-ranging and fascinating twelve years to complete my studies at Brown. My education has been expansive and inspiring. I have learned so much from all of you and from the extraordinary leadership of first Ruth Simmons and now Chris Paxson.

It was my father, Sidney Frank, who, with Ruth's guidance, created the Frank Scholars' endowment in 2005. It is that legacy that my father left to Brown, to me, and to the world that continues to shape me every day. I will continue to learn from the Sidney Frank Scholars for many decades to come. I admire these students, their intelligence and determination, their creativity and resourcefulness! What they have achieved through grit and determination before they even arrive at Brown is extraordinary! What they achieve at Brown is inspiring. On Sunday, twenty-six Frank Scholars will walk, dance, or run through the Van Wickle gates. They have majored in engineering and urban studies, in economics and biology. They will go out into the world and join the Frank Scholars who have preceded them and have already become doctors and lawyers, who have started their own not-for-profits, who are teachers and researchers.

I thank all of you and the incredible Brown community for making this possible!

With love,

Cathy

—

Cathy Frank Halstead
Trustee, 2005 – 2017

May 20, 2009

Dear Secretary Donald Hood,

I am submitting my resignation from the Brown Corporation effective June 30, 2009.

I would like to thank the Brown Alumni Association's Nominating Committee for nominating me to be a candidate as an Alumni trustee and I would also like to thank graduates of Brown for their votes and support.

These last 6 years have been the best for the University despite this recent downturn in the economy. We are a larger University with much improved academic, physical, and procedural infrastructures. During my time, the University has become a more effective research university, which is necessary for us to compete with our "peers" and to pursue more of an international footprint. We have made more of an effort to show the world that we are the best place to receive an undergraduate, graduate, or medical degree.

I will be forever grateful for the role that Brown has played in my life. You might find this hard to believe but I had never heard of Brown until I was a rising senior in high school in 1984. While participating in the Tougaloo College Summer Science Program, I met the President of Tougaloo College, Charlie Baldwin. Many of you may remember him as the University's chaplain. Many years later, whenever I would see him on Brown's campus, I would refer to him as President Baldwin. He would always show me a big smile. I think he liked the way that the title resonated.

As you know, Charlie Baldwin was a big supporter of the Brown-Tougaloo Partnership. As an undergraduate at Tougaloo, I did not fully appreciate the full scope of the history and the scope of the relationship. Over the years, I have seen how both institutions have benefited from their unique relationship of about 45 years. The undergraduates from both institutions have an opportunity to visit a different world right here in the US during the semester exchange programs. Participating students get a chance to go beyond their comfort zone and see things from a different perspective. I find comfort in knowing that the partnership will continue.

I would also like to thank Ruth Simmons for her extraordinary leadership of Brown. Her team is truly amazing. I wish I knew how she gets her cabinet to work so hard. My Corporation colleagues are the best and the brightest. I would like to challenge my fellow Corporation members to continue to work hard at asking the important questions and to make sure that undergraduates, graduate and medical students are given the best tools to succeed.

Playing a formal role in education has been a part of my family since the Emancipation of slaves. Education is the only thing that gives anyone the opportunity for access to choices or to move within and to improve a society. I am honored to have served and will continue to serve the interests of the University.

I will continue my relationship with Brown as the President-Elect of the Brown Medical School Alumni Association.

———

Galen V. Henderson
Doctor of Medicine, 1993
Trustee, 2003 – 2009, 2017 – 2023

United States Senate
WASHINGTON, D.C. 20510

May 3, 1979

Dear Mr. Justice:

Thank you for your letter of April 27th reminding me that my term as a Trustee of Brown University expires on June 30, 1979.

Accordingly, I herewith submit my resignation. May I add that I do so with regret, but as a Senator from Rhode Island and as the father of a Brown graduate, look forward to continuing to help the University in any way that I can, particularly vis-a-vis its relationship with the Federal Government.

May I add that in my capacity as Chairman of the Senate Subcommittee on Education, Arts and Humanities, I benefitted from my association with Brown University as it has made me more aware of the problems of our great private universities.

You may be sure that as Chairman of that particular subcommittee I shall continue to have a very real interest in the well-being of the University.

Warm regards.

Ever sincerely,

Claiborne Pell

The Honorable
Alfred H. Joslin
Secretary of the Corporation
Brown University
Providence, Rhode Island   02912

Claiborne Pell

Honorary Doctor of Laws, 1972

Trustee, 1974 – 1979

May 5, 2023

Richard Friedman
Secretary
Corporation Office
Brown University
Box 1887
Providence, 02912

Dear Mr. Friedman:

It has been a true honor to serve as a New Alumni Trustee on this Corporation. I want to express my deepest gratitude to you all, for I have found new friends and mentors, and to my peers, who entrusted me with the responsibility of fitting into these very big shoes 3 years ago.

I started my journey with Brown in 2013 rather naively. I remember being an ambitious senior in high school, who'd never been to the US, but was convinced that Brown was the place to be. Lucky for me, the early decision application worked out and my 17-year-old self could not have been more right. Being a student at Brown was magical. In true 'open curriculum' spirit, the learning journey was never limited to the confines of a classroom and there was never a dull moment, given the passion each professor brought to the table. I dared to dream bigger than ever. I had the chance to shadow India's former foreign secretary and to contribute to multiple publications all at the age of 19. Only at Brown!

Fast forward to graduation in 2018: all I could think as I walked out the Van Wickle Gates was, "I am not ready to leave this place." Naively again, I remember approaching Chris & Shankar with a job description for the position of an International Student Advisor, in hope that I could stick around another year. Lucky for me, it worked out and my 21-year-old self could not have been happier. After having championed the needs of international students as a student leader for 4 years, here I was piloting change! Being part of Brown's administration was inspiring. Our institution is ripe with inclusive thought leaders who are passionate to make this place the best version of itself that it can be. I had the chance to institutionalize change all at the age of 21. Only at Brown!

Three years ago, I remember getting an email from Russell Carey which, for a change, was *not* about a snow day! It was a request to interview for the New Alumni Trustee position. I took another leap of faith and lucky for me, it brought me to this wonderful community. Serving on the Corporation has been a dream! I am humbled to have been part of this group that committed to going need blind for international students. I've had the pleasure to share my passion for Brown with an amazing group of people and to influence positive change at this institution that I love so dearly all starting at the age of 23. Only at Brown, indeed!

I depart here proud of how far we've come and inspired by our commitment to our collective values. Lucky for me, I know this farewell is temporary, for I will forever be committed to serving this truly magical, inspiring, and dreamy place.

Ever true,

Divya Mehta

———

Divya Mehta
International Relations, 2018
Trustee, 2020 – 2023

I see Brown emerging into the public eye where its curriculum and qualities can be recognized on a nation-wide basis and the demand for attendance overwhelming . . .

—W. DUNCAN MacMILLAN II

————

Classics, 1953

Honorary Doctor of Laws, 1993

Trustee, 1974 – 1979, 1980 – 1985, 1988 – 1994, 1995 – 2001

"... That the College, under your Auspicious Government, may advance in every ornamental & Usefull Accomplishment, untill it shall attain to the Summit of Renown, and there stand unrivalled ..."

———

Darius Sessions
Corporator of The College
Trustee, 1770 – 1785

II 81

Gentlemen

It is well known to many of You, that
I have had the Honour of being a Member
of your Body, ever since the Establish:
:ment of the College Institution—
Indisposition of Body, hath, for several
Years past, prevented my Attendance,
And as that Impediment yet remains,
and but little prospect of a Removall,
I think it my Duty to withdraw, that
Room may be made for a more active
and usefull Member— I therefore
think proper, at this Time, to give You
Notice, that I do, now, resign said
Office— That the College, under
your Auspicious Government, may adv:
:ance in every ornamental & Usefull
Accomplishment, untill it shall attain
to the Summit of Renown, and there
stand unrivalled— Is the sincere
Wish and prayer of, Gentlemen,

Your respectfull Friend
& humble Servant

Darius Sessions—

Providence, Sepr 7th 1785

Students gather in front of the
Van Wickle Gates, 2021

How Brown Made Me, "Me"

To say that I was given at Brown the tools to live life and
serve the community would only be a partial truth. More
than that, Brown gave me, as I believe it has given all
of us, a framework with which to understand the world.

—CHARLES M. ROYCE

Economics, 1961
Trustee, 1989 – 1995, 1997 – 2003, 2004 – 2010
Fellow, 2010 – 2013

May 10, 2019

Dear Richard,

I hereby tender my resignation as trustee of the Brown Corporation.

What a six-year run this has been for the University! I'm very proud to have been part of this board.

Each trustee's letter conveys a special dignity that helps bind the Corporation to its purpose.

I'm here by chance. One of four children from a poor Cuban immigrant family in Miami, I was squeezed into the 1984 freshman class when, in August of 1980, I realized I was about to make the biggest mistake of my life. I called Brown admissions to ask if I could change my response and accept my offer of admission. You see, my parents had *made* me decline Brown—too liberal a school for a Cuban immigrant! The joy I felt from the quick "yes" on the phone was matched by relief when, after a prolonged silence following my asking if I could also get the same full-aid offer, I heard "we'll make it work out, please plan to join us in a few weeks." That call changed my life.

Brown literally *formed* me and my thinking, launched my family (I married my college sweetheart), and sustained us through the host of undergrad and grad friendships we made.

I cannot express what it is like to come from such humble beginnings and be "dropped" into all that is Brown. This still happens today. Brown *is* one of the bright rungs on the ladder of opportunity. I pray that access to Brown will always be offered to those who desire to make something of it.

I came to the Corporation to answer a call to service. When I reflect on that service, I take great pride in the work we have accomplished and am grateful to have had the opportunity to help steward this wonderful august institution to a place of greater excellence, diversity, inclusion, and comity. What I'll carry closest to my heart are the warm new friendships I have developed. I treasure the fun moments and adventures we've shared.

(Advice to new trustees: say "yes" to post-meeting Hope Club and Omni libations, and definitely do not miss February meetings when there is a chance to be snowed in!)

I am humbled by the generosity, concern, and love that are freely given when we come together. What we do affects so many young lives. This place is special.

Good luck all with the hard work ahead, and ever true,

José Estabil

————

José J. Estabil
Physics, 1984
Master of Science, Physics, 1988
Trustee, 2013 – 2019

May 2015

Ladies and Gentlemen:

Please bear with me a moment while I tell a story that is pertinent to everyone in this room. It's about a kid from South Central Los Angeles who didn't send an application fee with his application because he didn't have it. It's about a kid who sent in a money order to matriculate to the University because his parents didn't have a checking account. It's about a kid who sat curbside handcuffed on Wilshire Blvd because he "fit the description" and then decided he'd never "fit the description" again.

I matriculated into the University in September of 1979, in November of 1979 my mother suffered a severe stroke, I was financially unable to return home. To this day I don't know how the Dean of Students discovered my situation. However, he provided me with funds to go home for Christmas to see my mom. I will always be grateful to the University for that very large, small act.

Clearly the financial aid I received during my years at Brown allowed me to obtain my degree and go on to lead a productive life. Here's why this is important. People in this room during those times provided the underpinnings for that aid. The skills I acquired here allowed me to build a business that employed over 100 people. Those people bought houses and sent their children to colleges because of our success. The actions of the people in this room directly changed lives. I have a debt to this University that I can never repay. That is why it is with the utmost regret that I submit my resignation as a Trustee of Brown University today. Thank you from the bottom of my heart, you have nothing but my most sincere admiration.

Dorsey James

———

Dorsey M. James
Engineering, 1983
Trustee, 2009 – 2015

May 9, 2017

Dear Chancellor Mencoff, President Paxson, and Secretary Hood:

Please accept this letter as formal notice of my resignation from the Brown University Corporation, effective June 30, 2017. More importantly, I would like to express my sincere appreciation and gratitude for the opportunity to serve the University, its faculty and students these past six years. However, in reality, my thankfulness covers more than four decades.

I arrived at our university forty-five years ago during the Vietnam War from a classic midwestern farm state background. I had the attendant and appropriate levels of anxiety and doubt regarding my ability to navigate the challenges of the academic rigor as well as the more liberal mindset. I could not have imagined how my four years here as a student would transform and prepare me for the life with which I have been so blessed. I am exceptionally grateful to Brown for helping me become the person I am today and humbled to think what course my life might have taken in the absence of my years on College Hill.

Equally, I never imagined I would have the good fortune to spend the last six years in the company of such extraordinarily wise, talented, diverse, and committed fellow Corporation members. Working together to move Brown forward on behalf of our outstanding students and faculty, with the likes of President Paxson and my good friend, fraternity brother, and graduate school roommate Sam Mencoff, has been a unique honor. I am optimistic that Brown University will continue to advance in many constructive and prudent ways.

I have been forever enriched by the Brown experience. I hope in some small way I have returned the favor by always trying to be of the best service to this great institution. It deserves nothing less.

With profound gratitude, I remain Ever True and Ever Grateful,

Kevin A. Mundt
Economics, 1976
Honorary Doctor of Humane Letters, 2023
Trustee, 2011 – 2017

Brown has enabled me, as it has countless others, to explore. To explore computer science, to explore what it means to be educated, to explore what it means to be an American, to explore ancient and new texts and theories, to explore how a university leads and responds to societal change, to explore how to create the future, how to create new knowledge, and how to create lifelong friends.

—EILEEN M. RUDDEN

———

American Civilization, 1972
Trustee, 2003 – 2009

"The welfare of the institution and its continued usefulness to society demand that the broad and liberal principles of its foundation should be applied in harmony with changed conditions."

—The 1945 edition of the Charter of Brown University with Amendments and Notes

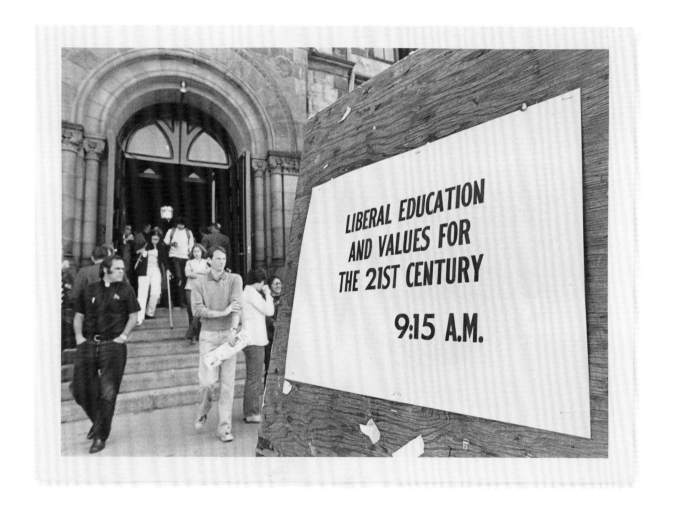

Outside Sayles Hall, 1977

May 2021

Dear Rich,

Arriving at Brown as an incoming freshman the summer of 1994 I had absolutely no idea how the experiences I was about to encounter would help to shape and prepare me for the next 27 years.

It was at Brown where I for the first time ever made a decision about what classes I would or would not take. It was at Brown where I first experienced people with extraordinary wealth and privilege. It was at Brown where I first experienced people who identified themselves as socialists or communists. It was at Brown where I first had real conversations with someone who identified themselves as gay even though I grew up with an older gay brother. It was at Brown where I first learned that talking too much can get you in trouble.

It never occurred to me that over the 4 years at Brown that I was really learning about myself. What was my world view? What are my passions? How do I identify success? Important life lessons that serve me to this day as a public servant.

I cannot thank Brown enough for the confidence to walk into any given situation (and I deal with many different situations) knowing that whatever I am about to encounter I have seen some version of it before during my time at Brown. Education is more than what you learn when sitting in a classroom and Brown gets it. Brown isn't a good fit for everyone but when it fits it is a perfect match.

I never in a million years would have thought that I would be asked to sit on the Board of Trustees at an institution like Brown University. I am the son of Caribbean immigrants, who didn't graduate from junior high school in their respective countries. When notified that I would be selected as an Alumni Trustee I did everything I could to prepare to be a resource.

I have very much enjoyed my committee assignments and I want to thank everyone who played a role in helping me to gain a real look into the inner workings of Brown. Whether it was Campus Life or the Finance Committee I was able to give my perspective to help Brown manage the University. Everything from the strategic sessions, the informal dinners, the relationships I have been able to form have been part of this amazing 6 year experience.

Literally, where has the time gone.

I wish I wasn't transitioning off the board in a year where we experienced Covid-19 that ushered in the Zoom era while at the same time running in a taxing citywide campaign that leaves me with very little time for other important priorities but I am happy to know that I will be able to serve as a trustee emeritus and stay engaged with the University that has given me so much. I will spend my life trying to repay Brown in anyways that I can, big or small. Thanks.

Sincerely,

Brian Benjamin

————

Brian A. Benjamin
Public Policy and American Institutions, 1998
Trustee, 2015 – 2021

I arrived on campus in 1983—I knew no one; I was intimidated by all the NY private school kids . . . I had been on one airplane in my life and was the furthest thing from "worldly;" I was on significant financial aid, with maximum loans and work requirements . . . I could not have imagined how four years would transform me, open my mind to the world . . .

—TODD A. FISHER

———

Biology, 1987
Trustee, 2013 – 2019

May 17, 2019

Dear Corporation,

Thank you. Thank you. Thank you. Two years have flown by!

I still remember my first Corporation meeting in October 2017. Even among a group of fellow incoming Trustees—individuals that I admire—I wondered how I could have an impact and if it would be too nerve-wracking to speak up. After Jerome's cold call at my first Bacaro dinner, I knew that speaking up would be essential. And speak up, I did, with the support of so many of you. There are so many people to thank, and I know I can't list all of you or this letter would be too long; but please know that this letter is a thank you to each and every one of you.

Particularly, thank you Chris for your courageous leadership and support as I joined the Corporation. Thank you Joan for your endless mentorship, both to me and my sister. Pamela, thank you so much for inviting me to speak on my first panel discussion. Thank you to all the Corporation members that guided my graduate school application process—I am the first in my family to attend business school and couldn't have navigated the process without your support.

Resigning from the Corporation always felt bittersweet. What a privilege to serve for two years, but time flies. Over the past few months, I worried about how I could continue to give back to Brown as a Trustee Emeritus. However, I want to share a brief story from my experience at my current school in Boston, not to draw a competition between the two schools but to point to an experience that reinforced the value of my Brown experience and the never-ending relationship that I will have with Brown and the Corporation.

This Spring, Black students at Harvard Business School were targeted with a series of hateful, slur-filled, and life-threatening emails from an anonymous group. Tangentially, students organizing around diversity and inclusion in admissions at Harvard Kennedy School received similar threats. As a student at both schools, I felt distress from my safety feeling compromised with limited support from university leadership or school-led discourse on the topic. Eventually, minority students organized discussions within sections and cohorts to discuss the events and how Harvard could do better. A Harvard Kennedy School student mentioned that students proposed a Diversity and Inclusion plan with limited reply from the administration about the possibility of creating one—not a "No" or a "Maybe;" simply no channel for even having a discussion. During one of the meetings, a classmate asked "Who is Harvard forming us to be?" and I was disappointed to observe that none of my students had an answer—myself included.

However, I raised my hand . . . because despite feeling lost about who my graduate school was forming me to be, I knew what Brown helped me become.

Brown encouraged me to be a critical thinker. Brown pushed me to name difficult issues and address them head on. Most importantly, Brown pushed me to inspire change and growth among my communities. It did not matter if it was a pre-orientation discussion on summer reading, an Africana Studies course on Pan-Africanism, or a Corporation meeting years after my time at Brown. Those core tenets run through.

Suddenly, I am informing my classmates about Brown's DIAP. I am sharing my experiences on the Corporation as a 27-year-old, surrounded by inspiring individuals who show me how their Brown experiences still shape them today as trailblazers in their respective fields. I spoke about the breakfasts, evening discussions, and coffee chats that Corporation members hold with current students—unheard of at Harvard. And lo and behold! My sadness about leaving the Corporation is met with pride. I get to spend the rest of my life representing Brown in so many ways, and the opportunities and experiences I've shared with all of you inspire me as a hopeful future leader. I have never been more proud to be a member of the Corporation, and look forward to being an engaged Trustee Emeritus.

All the best,

Chichi Anyoku

———

Chichi Anyoku
Economics and Latin American and Caribbean Studies, 2014
Trustee, 2017 – 2019

May 2019

Dear Mr. Friedman,

My entry into this room began with a phone call I received while sitting in my childhood home nestled deep in the Appalachian Mountains from then Chancellor Tisch stating matter of factly, "So I hear you are good at time management, would you like to join the Corporation?" The rest is history.

This experience has simultaneously been everything and nothing like I had thought it would be. I am so fortunate to have been welcomed into a group that has been the first to celebrate my accomplishments with me and shout them from the rooftops. This group has also been there to console me in times of immense grief.

And yet, despite all of the positive experiences and encounters that I will take away from my time as a trustee, I have also experienced substantial dissonance. Dissonance in being part of the leadership structure of an institution whose very founding was from the profits of bodies who look like mine. Dissonance from having critical institutional conversations primarily in a building that was laid brick by brick by enslaved Black people. The original charter of Brown University written in 1764, and its subsequent amendments, never had a place for me at this institution and certainly not in this room. Yet 250 years later, I, an American Descendent of Slaves, granddaughter of a sharecropper, daughter of blue-collar workers in Appalachia, have ascended to the Brown Corporation. Through the last three years I have often asked myself what does it mean to govern an institution whose founding was fundamentally based on oppression and exclusion?

Ultimately, I am grateful to have witnessed and taken part in Brown learning out loud in the process of becoming a more inclusive environment. The Brown when I arrived as a first-year in 2012 felt scary and inaccessible. Having witnessed the founding of the U-FLI Center [Undocumented, First-Generation College and Low-Income Student Center], the creation of the DIAP [The Diversity and Inclusion Action Plan], the renaming of Page-Robinson Hall, the Brown that exists now, finally feels like home. There is still much room to grow, but I am so fulfilled by the students who have pushed the institution to be better and subsequently how far Brown has come.

I am privileged to have served dutifully in this role for three years, but I also recognize that Brown was equally privileged to have had me.

Ever true,

Mya Roberson

———

Mya L. Roberson
Public Health, 2016
Trustee, 2016 – 2019, 2022 – 2028

Over the course of my time as an undergraduate,
I found my intellectual voice and the values
which have guided me throughout my career.

—CRAIG E. BARTON

————

Semiotics, 1978
Trustee, 2012 – 2017
Fellow, 2017 – 2019

Student protest, University Hall, 1989

Always an Old Brown, Always a New Brown

I thought back to my first board meeting where I
pondered the fact that as a Brown trustee, I was now
officially part of the establishment and not on the
outside of University Hall, protesting some earth-
shattering issues. That revelation scared me a little . . .

—DEBRA L. LEE

———

Political Science, 1976
Honorary Doctor of Humane Letters, 2014
Trustee, 1994 – 2001, 2006 – 2012

JOEL DAVIS

May 15, 1973

Honorable Alfred H. Joslin
Associate Justice of the Supreme Court
Supreme Court
Providence, Rhode Island 02903

Dear Al:

According to approved procedure, I am hereby tendering my resignation from the Corporation effective June 30, 1973.

To say that these five years have been typical of any other similar period in Brown's history would be somewhat ludicrous. Merely to look back on the state of the University in 1968 provides a rather interesting perspective.

President Heffner, along with two undergraduates by the names of Maxwell and Magaziner, was trying to deal with campus unrest, including such inconsequential items as minority representation, curricular reform and ROTC. One of my first A & E Meetings was held in front of two hundred uninvited students. A thirty-four year old Trustee was then considered young. Blacks were barely noticeable on the campus. Pembroke was a girl's school. Co-ed living was something you read about at Berkeley. The Medical School was merely a dream. There was no graduate dorm, no Jackie Mattfield, no List Art Building, no Science Library, no Bryant Campus, and no artificial lake opposite Meehan Auditorium. Probably the only campus institution not overtly affected by the past five years was the Football Team. In short the changes which have taken place have been dramatic; no doubt the most dramatic in Brown's 205 year proud history.

During these past five years I have been privileged to serve on this Corporation, including representation on the Search Committee responsible for the selection of President Hornig, and for the past two years on the A & E Committee and Chairman of the Committee on Budget and Finance. I would not exchange this experience for all the full price ELLERY QUEEN subscriptions in the world.

But time dictates a change, a change which is good for Brown, good for the Corporation and good for the individual involved. To my fellow Corporation members I extend my sincere best wishes as you face the new problems and opportunities in the years ahead.

Sincerely,

Joel Davis

jd:sf

Joel Davis

American Civilization, 1956

Trustee, 1968 – 1973

Edward Sulzberger

October 6, 1971

Mr. John Nicholas Brown
Secretary of the Corporation
Brown University
Providence, Rhode Island

Dear Mr. Brown:

Death, taxes, and resignations from the Board of Trustees are inevitable, and I hereby submit my resignation to become effective June 30, 1972.

It is difficult for me to believe that seven years will have elapsed since I became a Trustee of the University in 1965. The fact that the time has gone so rapidly is indicative of the benefits received, and the pleasure enjoyed during this period.

It is interesting to note the parallel that exists between the National Government and Brown University from 1965 to the present time. The United States had more than one President, so too, Brown University. Our way of life has changed from one of peaceful quiet and prosperity to one of dissatisfaction, turmoil, and economic distress. Brown University has experienced changes of a similar nature. Yet look how Brown fares today compared with our country. The result of Brown's policies has produced a strong and united University, which is facing the future with confidence.

What I'm trying to say is that our University should run the Government.

I sincerely appreciate the opportunity of having been able to serve on the Brown Board. My loyalty has never wavered, and my services will always be available.

My best wishes for continued University prosperity and success.

Sincerely

Edward Sulzberger

ES/gm

Edward Sulzberger
Bachelor of Philosphy, 1929
Trustee, 1965 – 1972

I have been privileged to serve on the Corporation
during the term of one of Brown's greatest presidents,
whose straight-backed leadership has guided this
university with confidence, clarity, and distinction
during a period punctuated—perhaps uniquely—by
extremes of economic prosperity and challenge.

—SAMUEL M. MENCOFF

————

Anthropology, 1978
Chancellor, 2016 – 2024
Trustee, 2003 – 2009, 2016 – 2024
Fellow, 2009 – 2016

May 24, 1970

Dear Mr. Brown:

I have your letter of April 22, 1970 and, being duly reminded, hereby submit my resignation as a Trustee of Brown University. Upon my election to the Corporation in 1963 you advised me that I would hear from you again in seven years' time. Unfortunately you have a good memory.

The last seven years have provided a real insight into the tremendous contribution Brown is making to education and to citizenship in our country and in our community. I only regret that I am retiring in such an exciting period of challenge and of change.

My tour of duty as a Trustee has been most rewarding to me. It has in fact accomplished a heretofore unheard of biological event—the conversion of a bulldog into a bear.

Sincerely yours,

Fredrick Lippitt

———

Fredrick Lippitt
Honorary Doctor of Laws, 1977
Trustee, 1963 – 1970
Fellow, 1979 – 2005

January 19, 1974

Dear Don:

It has been my privilege to participate in the affairs of the University since 1956 and I have done so with deep satisfaction. The duties of my engagement have come during a period of notable change and development. In addition, I have enjoyed the company of earnest people while working toward the worthy ends of our institution.

However, I have reached the conclusion that this is the appropriate time for me to resign from the Board of Fellows. I submit my resignation to you for presentation to the Board and ask that it become effective as of the Commencement meeting. I am convinced that my request is in the best interest of the University.

I look forward to seeing you at the February meetings and send you my warmest wishes for useful results.

Sincerely,

Mrs. Bleike Sheldon Reed

Dr. Donald F. Hornig,
President
Brown University
Providence
Rhode Island

Doris Brown Reed

Social Science, 1927

Honorary Doctor of Laws, 1962

Trustee, 1956 – 1962, 1963 – 1969

Fellow, 1969 – 1974

1968 was an extraordinarily tumultuous year . . .
College campuses throughout America
and beyond had exploded in opposition to
the Vietnam war and racial injustice.

During this same period, creative, insightful, and
enlightened initiatives laid the groundwork for Brown's
ascendance as one of the "hottest" universities . . .

Ira Magaziner's brilliant innovation—the New
Curriculum—was a profound development. Also, the
peaceful 1968 Walkout by Black Students at a period
during which Columbia, Cornell, Michigan,
Cal-Berkeley, Wisconsin, Stony Brook, and numerous other
institutions were embroiled in extraordinarily volatile
confrontations. These circumstances set the Brown
brand apart, as a forward-thinking, ingenious leader.

Brown's special reputation was well-earned. The
Walkout of '68 and the Civil Rights Movement led
to the admission of the largest class of African
Americans in the history of the University.

The number of African Americans enrolled in my Class
of '73 was second, only to the number of Blacks enrolled
in Harvard's Class of '73. The Walkout also led to the
matriculation of other persons of color and women
in numbers that far exceeded the numbers that had
been previously accepted by Brown and Pembroke.

—PRESTON C. TISDALE

———

Public Policy Making, 1973
Trustee, 2015 – 2021

Student demonstration, 1975

As was the case with my undergraduate experience,
I have learned a great deal during my tenure as a
trustee . . . much of it not part of the "curriculum."

—BENJAMIN V. LAMBERT

———

Art, 1960
Trustee, 1983 – 1989

EUGENE C. SWIFT

May 5, 1971

Brown University
Providence, R. I. 02912

Attention - Mr. John Nicholas Brown
Secretary of the Corporation

Dear John:

My term as Trustee ends June 30th. I
have appreciated the opportunity to serve and
sincerely wish the members of the Corporation the
best of luck in the handling of the problems of
the 70's. While there will be many frustrations,
it will be an exciting period.

I expect to be called upon if there is
any way in the judgment of others that I can help
the University.

Sincerely,

Gene

ECS:me

Eugene C. Swift
History, 1942
Trustee, 1966 – 1971

Students protest ROTC in the Corporation Room, 1969

Commencement on the College Green, 1966

Women at Brown: Beyond Pembroke

During my tenure, two major decisions were
made which have had great impact—namely,
the merger of Pembroke with the College and
the establishment of the Medical School . . .

—BETTE LIPKIN BROWN

———

Psychology, 1946
Trustee, 1970 – 1975

Editor's Note: Originally called The Women's College in Brown University and renamed Pembroke
College in Brown University in 1928, Pembroke was officially merged with The College in 1971.
However, women were always awarded degrees from Brown University, starting with the first two
women graduates in 1894.

WARWICK, RHODE ISLAND 02888

June 22, 1965

Dear Mr. Brown:

Thank you for your letter of June 5.

I am keenly aware of the honor that
is mine in becoming the first Alumnae Trustee
on the Corporation of Brown University --
and equally aware of the responsibility involved. It is my earnest hope that I shall
be able to make a worthwhile contribution
during my term of service.

I understand that the term is for
five years, and in the spring of 1970 I shall
be careful to tender my resignation before it
has to be "solicited."

Sincerely yours,

Elizabeth Goodale Kenyon '39

Mr. John Nicholas Brown
Secretary of the Corporation
Brown University
Providence, Rhode Island 02912

Elizabeth Goodale Kenyon

History, 1939

Trustee, 1965 – 1970

Members of the Corporation of Brown University, 1951, including the first
woman trustee, Anna Canada Swain 1911 (bottom right).

May 11, 1988
Howard R. Swearer, President
Brown University
Providence, Rhode Island

Dear Howard,

When I wrote my resignation as a trustee in the spring of 1977, I expressed my gratitude
for the opportunity to have a second education at Brown University. Apparently the
Fellows thought I had not yet mastered my lessons. In the fall of 1977 they asked me
to join them for a "postgraduate" course. This third attempt by Brown University to
educate me (and me to educate it) has been challenging as well as interesting. I have
especially enjoyed the privilege of being the first woman to serve as an officer of the
Corporation. Now, hoping that I have finally mastered the course of instruction, I submit
my resignation as a member of the Board of Fellows of Brown University, effective June
30, 1988.

I want to express my gratitude to all the members of the Corporation, the administration
and the faculty who have made my years on the Brown Corporation such a pleasure. I
look forward to continuing contacts with many of you and to continuing service to the
University as I become a Fellow Emerita.

Sincerely yours,

Ruth B. Ekstrom

———

Ruth Burt Ekstrom
Psychology, 1953
Honorary Doctor of Laws, 1988
Secretary, 1982 – 1988
Trustee, 1972 – 1977
Fellow, 1977 – 1988

October 3, 1976

Judge Alfred H. Joslin, Secretary
The Corporation
Brown University
Providence, R.I. 02912

Dear Al;

It is with regret that I submit to you my resignation as Alumnae Trustee, effective June, 1977.

In retrospect, I view my term with satisfaction and some misgivings. I am troubled by the opportunities I missed to innovate and by the things I might have said, but didn't. On the other hand, those involvements in which I have participated have heightened my awareness of Brown's strengths and frailties and have made me a far better spokesman in her behalf.

My social attitudes have changed as a result of my Corporation membership and my consciousness in regard to women in our co-educational institution and the larger society has been sharpened. I am grateful for the opportunity to serve in this, my last year, as a member of the Corporation committee to Study the Status of Women at Brown.

I shall miss being closely involved with you in the upcoming Swearer era. From all indications our new president should provide challenging and productive leadership for this Corporation as it faces the 1980's.

My warmest thanks go to the alumnae and alumni who made it possible for me to serve Brown at this privileged level.

Best wishes, always.

Sincerely,

Ruth

(Ruth Harris Wolf, '41)

Ruth Harris Wolf

German, 1941

Honorary Doctor of Laws, 1981

Trustee, 1972 – 1977

3 October 1975

The Honorable Alfred H. Joslin
Secretary of the Corporation
Brown University
Providence, R.I. 02912

Dear Al:

In compliance with the "firm but gentle" directive
I received upon my election to the Corporation, I
herewith submit my resignation as of June 1976.

Since, by tradition, it appears that I am given this
opportunity to share reflections on my term as a
trustee, I find many numbers and dates coming to
mind. June 1976 marks not only my completion of
five years as an Alumnae Trustee but also my thirty-
fifth reunion year and my thirtieth year as a Brown
University faculty wife. I may never have left home
but, fortunately, Mother Brunonia in the true liberal
arts tradition provides unending opportunities for
emotional and intellectual growth.

I have always been mindful that I was the thirteenth
woman elected to this Corporation; the number has
been significant to me not for reasons of supersti-
tion but because of my personal awe that I should be
one of these pioneer figures. Indeed, of the twenty
women elected to this Corpration in the two hundred
and eleven years of the University, all save one are
still living. That fact is indicative of the new and
recent role women are playing in the University's
governance. I hope that I may continue to bring to
the attention of the Corporation the names of
capable women to serve in the future.

I have felt particularly fortunate during my term
because I have been privileged to serve on those
committees which interested me the most and which
dealt with matters in which I felt some competence:
the University Libraries, the Student Life, and the

Edwards' Study Committee on the Alumni/Alumnae
merger. One of my concerns for many years has been
the need for a new theater facility, and it has been
very gratifying recently to work toward this effort
because of the Kresge Challenge Grant.

I hope I have been an effective ambassador of the
University to all constituencies: students, faculty,
administration, graduates, and even that world outside.
I intend to continue my efforts and, I trust, doing
so will make me worthy of the honor you have bestowed
upon me.

Respectfully,

Sophie

Sophia Schaffer Blistein

Sophia Schaffer Blistein
English, 1941
Trustee, 1971 – 1976

May 2016

Dear Don –

At this time, it is my bittersweet duty to respectfully resign from the Brown University Corporation. It has been a privilege and an honor to serve this University under the extraordinary leadership of Presidents Ruth Simmons and Chris Paxson.

When Thomas Perez became the US Secretary of Labor, I told my son Jeffrey (who was then a student at Brown) that Tom and I used to hitch rides home together from Brown for December break, as neither of us could afford to fly. My son asked me if I could tell that Tom was destined for greatness and I realized that back then, I didn't know what greatness was.

You see, I grew up in the suburbs of Buffalo and attended a large public high school where those who actually went to college rarely left New York State. I was fortunate to have discovered, applied, and been admitted to Brown and, in 1979, I became the first student from my high school to attend Brown. Although it's strange to admit now, I came to Brown without any career aspirations, figuring that I'd get an excellent education and be a housewife, just like my mom and all the other women I knew. We all have dreams as to where life will take us; I didn't know how to dream that big. But Brown opened my eyes to opportunities I never imagined were possible and allowed me to pursue a life I could not even have contemplated.

I worked hard during my time at Brown, holding multiple jobs to help put myself through school, but also had amazing experiences, including being a TA in CS 51 for Andy van Dam, studying art and theater for a semester in London, and working for Ira Magaziner as my Senior ISP. I was fortunate to find terrific internships, one summer for IBM in Boulder, Colorado (the summer IBM unveiled its first PC), and the next for a small software company in Boston owned by a Brown alum. My mentor and boss at BGS Systems was a woman who, for the first time, challenged me to aspire to greatness as a professional woman, which had a profound impact on me. These internships helped to propel me to Goldman Sachs, where I spent 15 fabulous years.

So raising funds to support students, particularly those who need financial assistance to attend Brown, and working to develop a program to help students find life-enhancing internships, were two areas of personal interest to me. My six years on the Corporation have provided me with the opportunity to make great strides in both of these areas.

Those of you who knew me when I began my term on the Corporation may remember me with my leg in a tall pink cast trying to navigate Brown's campus on my scooter through the ice and snow. Thankfully, that is now all behind me. The opportunities I have had—co-chairing the Brown Annual Fund with Sam Mencoff, helping to create BrownConnect with Genine Fidler, and working to build the volunteer pipeline with Lauren Zalaznick—have been meaningful and engaging, and I am pleased with the progress we have made on many fronts. Through this work, I have been impressed with the generosity of our alumni, parents, and friends and their willingness to contribute to Brown in so many ways.

As my tenure on the Corporation comes to a close, I would like to thank you for allowing me to serve this wonderful University. As I move to become an emerita Corporation member, I certainly plan to continue my work with BrownConnect and hopefully other initiatives. This University has had a profound impact on my life and that of my family. I will be forever grateful and will remain Ever True and dedicated to helping to further the success and excellence of Brown.

Very truly yours,

Andrea Terzi Baum '83, P'15, P'18

—————

Andrea Terzi Baum
Computer Science, 1983
Trustee, 2010 – 2016

Just five years ago I visited my father, whom I loved,
who was dying. Knowing his love for and interest
in his daughters, even in the worst of times, I said,
"Well, Daddy, I have some good news. The president
of Brown called yesterday and asked me to serve
as trustee of the University. Isn't that exciting?"

"It is, dearie," came the reply from the pillow. "But
what makes them think you have that much money?"

— JUDITH CAMERON WHITTAKER

———

American Civilization, 1959
Trustee, 1977 – 1982

October 1, 1963

Dear Mr. Brown:

Thankyou for your kind letter reminding me that my term as a Trustee of Brown University expires at the close of the meeting on October 19.

In submitting my resignation as of the above date, I would like to take this opportunity to thank the Corporation for the privilege of serving as a trustee during this seven year period. I consider it to have been not only a great honor but also one of the most rewarding experiences of my life.

Needless to say, the expiration of my term as trustee will not in the slightest degree dininish my interest in Brown and Pembroke. As I watch from the sidelines the inevitable progress of this great University, please be assured that I stand ready to help, should the occasion ever arise that I may be of service.

Yours sincerely,

Mrs. J. Murray Beardsley

Mr. John Nicholas Brown
Secretary to the Corporation
Brown University
Providence 12, Rhode Island

Sarah Morse Beardsley

Bachelor of Arts, 1918

Trustee, 1956 – 1963

> "With sincere appreciation for the opportunity to serve
> Brown University as the fifth woman trustee . . ."

Providence, R.I.
May 8, 1967.

Mr. John Nicholas Brown, Secretary
Brown University
Providence, R.I.

Dear Mr. Brown:

In reply to your recent letter reminding me that my term as a Trustee of Brown University expires at the close of the Commencement meeting I

[... my
... lege, an
... to serve
... tstanding,
... this period
... growth
... nterest,
... continue
... tion for the
... n University
... ee,]

Very sincerely yours,
Pauline A. Hughes
(Mrs. William Newton Hughes)

Pauline Barrows Hughes

Bachelor of Arts, 1921

Trustee, 1960 – 1967

May 19, 2005

Secretary Wendy J. Strothman
Box 1887
Brown University
Providence, RI 02912

Dear Secretary Strothman, Chancellor Robert, President Simmons, and Members of the Brown Corporation:

About two years ago, a trustee's letter of resignation was presented at the Corporation meeting and when his name was read at the end, the collective response from all present was "Who?" I can only hope that my service as a trustee has been a bit more helpful as well as memorable.

It is with great sadness that I now tender my own resignation letter and say goodbye to this very fine group of interesting, dedicated, honorable, and hardworking people who share my love for Brown. I feel honored to have served with all of you in our joint effort to enhance the quality of education at Brown and to advance the good name and stature of this remarkable educational institution. Moreover, I feel particularly honored to have been a part of the governing body that had the good sense to hire Madame President Ruth Simmons. Of all the substantive votes I cast during my six-year tenure, that clearly was the most important.

May all of your future governance deliberations continue to be inspired by your collective wisdom and experience. I look forward to seeing you at upcoming Brown events.

Sincerely,

O. Rogeriee Thompson

_____

O. Rogeriee Thompson
English and American Literature, 1973
Honorary Doctor of Laws, 2021
Trustee, 1999 – 2005
Fellow, 2013 – 2017

May 20, 2004

Ms. Wendy J. Strothman
Secretary of the Corporation
Brown University
Box 1887
Providence, RI 02912

Dear Wendy:

This is not a letter I want to write. Fellows and trustees never want to write these letters. (What never? No, never. What never? Well … hardly ever.)

I have loved Brown and Pembroke from the day I first set foot on campus as a 17 year old freshman. This place (as Charlie Baldwin always called it when he was praying for us) welcomed me then and still does every time I again set foot on campus.

Being asked to serve on the Brown Corporation was an honor and a privilege, and to be asked back after everyone knew me was an even greater honor and privilege.

I have loved being a member of the Brown Corporation. I have cherished the opportunity to serve with great Presidents, of whom Ruth Simmons is one, and great Chancellors (I still miss Charlie Tillinghast and Dick Salomon, but their successors – Al, Artie, and Steve – have written their own estimable chapters in Brown's book). I am especially grateful for the many friendships forged in this Corporation room and the other venues in which we meet.

My head says I must tender my resignation and I hereby do so, effective June 30, 2004. My heart wishes it weren't so.

Sincerely,

Nancy L. Buc

Nancy L. Buc
American Civilization, 1965
Honorary Doctor of Laws, 1994
Trustee, 1973 – 1978, 1998 – 2004
Fellow, 1980 – 1992

My thanks to staff, faculty, and fellow members of
the Corporation for the privilege of viewing first-hand
the intricate balancing of issues, ideals, and reality
which goes into the operation of a great university.

— JEAN MacPHAIL WEBER

———

Art, 1954
Trustee, 1983 – 1988

I have gained much more than I could offer. And who could overlook that additional delight, the opportunity to wear that slightly jaunty, somewhat droll, always festive, and very Brunonian "Beefeater" hat?

—SALLY HILL COOPER

———

German, 1952
Trustee, 1979 – 1984

Commencement, 2018

September 24, 197[5]

Dear Al —

This letter is hardly to be
compared with an historic
letter of resignation that was
written last August — Regrettably,
however, it marks the end of
a very special opportunity I
had — to serve as an Alumnae
Trustee — Even though my term
ends on June 30, 1975, I shall
continue to work for my
Alma Mater with interest and

Reluctantly, Resigned

Your pastime—reading letters of resignation—has
been an enjoyable part of each fall meeting. Now
that my time has come, it no longer is enjoyable.

—CHRISTINE DUNLAP FARNHAM

———

English, 1948
Trustee, 1976 – 1981

May 8, 2009

Dear Don,

Your letter requesting my resignation from the Corporation puts me in mind of a story.

There was a successful family business, a manufacturing company in the Midwest, and one day the son suggested to his father that they should have a mandatory retirement policy. The father thought it was a good idea but stipulated that it would apply to everyone with the exception of himself. The son was about 40 at the time, and his father was already past 60, so he was perfectly satisfied with the outcome of the discussion. The years went by and the father remained in robust health and at the helm of the company, to the increasing frustration of the now aging son. Sure enough, on his 65th birthday, his father doddered into his office and, after wishing him a happy birthday, presented him with a gold watch and told him it was time to retire. The son thought he was kidding. But no. It was a policy the son himself had proposed, and his father would hold him to it. True story.

As a proponent of term limits for the Corporation, I now know something of what the son must have felt. How many times over the years did I quip to Steve Robert and others something about life sentences being a bad idea? Alas, they are. So, it is with regret, nostalgia, sadness, and firm conviction in the soundness of the policy that I hereby resign for the last time from the Brown Corporation.

Over the past 23 years, it has been my privilege to serve under a succession of extraordinary Chancellors and Presidents, Dick and Howard, Al, Artie, and Greg, Steve, Tom, and Ruth. It has also been my pleasure to get to know and count as friends many fellow members of the Corporation. All of you, living and otherwise, have my enduring gratitude and unbounded admiration for all you have done and will do to further enhance Brown's usefulness and reputation in the world.

Sincerely,

Timothy C. Forbes

———

Timothy C. Forbes
Semiotics, 1976
Honorary Doctor of Humane Letters, 1996
Trustee, 1988 – 1994, 1995 – 1997
Fellow, 1998 – 2009

Members of the Corporation of Brown University, 1933, including
Allyn L. Brown 1905 (fourth row, seventh from left).

JUN 26 1963

June 25, 1963

President Barnaby C. Keeney
Brown Corporation
Brown University
Providence-12, R.I.

Dear President Keeney:

I hereby tender my resignation as a Life Trustee of the
Corporation of Brown University to take effect at the close
of the October 1963 meeting.

Brown has been generous indeed to me.   After a term as
Alumni Trustee from 1930 to 1936, the Corporation elected
me a Life Trustee on October 7, 1939, making an aggregate
total of thirty years which I have served. God willing, I
shall become eighty years old on October 26, 1963.   As I
have explained to you as President of the Corporation, I have
come increasingly to feel that for me to continue a Trustee
precludes the appointment of a younger man possessed of the
attributes, energies and potentialities which will more fully
afford to you the kind of support which your effective and
dynamic leadership needs and so richly deserves.

It is a high honor to be a member of the Brown Corporation and
the associations and friendships incident to it have been a
source of great pleasure and satisfaction to me.   Membership
on no other board with which I have been identified has given
me the true enjoyment and satisfaction realized in being one
of the Brown Corporation.   Loath as I am to terminate this
cherished association, I sincerely trust that you and all of
my fellow members of the Corporation will construe my action
as it is intended, as evidence not of a waning but rather of
an ever growing loyalty to Brown.

                    Very sincerely,

                    Allyn L. Brown.

Allyn L. Brown

Bachelor of Arts, 1905

Trustee, 1931 – 1937, 1938 – 1963

JUL 2 8 1966

July 27, 1966

Dear Mr. President,

I suppose a lifetime job is the best way of
achieving the goal of social security.

I'm thrilled with my new lifetime job as a
Fellow of Brown, but I am also quite aware of the risks
of staying too long, especially since indispensability
sets in about the same time as senility. It must
become increasingly hard to know when to quit, and I
want to quit while I am still ahead.

May I ask you to consider that you now hold
my resignation as a Fellow with complete authority to
make it effective whenever you believe such action to
be in the best interests of the University. I hope I
shall know enough to do it myself, but I may not.

This does not signify any change in my intention
to do all that I can to further the interests of Brown
and to support you in your Presidency.

Sincerely,

Gordon Cadwgan

Dr. Ray Heffner, President
Brown University
Providence, Rhode Island

Gordon E. Cadwgan

Economics, 1936

Honorary Doctor of Laws, 1966

Trustee, 1959 – 1966

Fellow, 1966 – 1983

Your much dreaded letter requesting my resignation
arrived. I was tempted to put it in the "should
do" pile rather than the "must do" pile, then
it might never have seen the light of day.

—MARIE J. LANGLOIS

———

Economics, 1964
Honorary Doctor of Laws, 1992
Treasurer, 1988 – 1992
Vice Chancellor, 1998 – 2007
Trustee, 1980 – 1985, 1988 – 1992, 1998 – 2007
Fellow, 1992 – 1998

UNIVERSITY OF CALIFORNIA
SAN FRANCISCO MEDICAL CENTER

BERKELEY • DAVIS • IRVINE • LOS ANGELES • RIVERSIDE • SAN DIEGO • SAN FRANCISCO SANTA BARBARA • SANTA CRUZ

SCHOOL OF MEDICINE
NEUROLOGY SERVICE

Please address reply to the undersigned at
UNIVERSITY OF CALIFORNIA SERVICE
SAN FRANCISCO GENERAL HOSPITAL
SAN FRANCISCO, CALIFORNIA 94110

May 3, 1974

Judge Alfred H. Joslin
Secretary of the Corporation
Brown University
Providence RI 02912

Your Honor:

It is with a reluctant sense of inevitability, just as one resists
the inexorable march of time, that I tender my resignation, effective
June 30, 1974, in accordance with the terms of my election as Trustee.

It has been my privilege to have participated in the birth, growth and
development of the Medical School Program. In creating this Program,
Brown University faced the challenge of "institutional responsibility"
by meeting the needs of a larger community and yet maintaining high
standards of scholarship. This action sustains my belief in the via-
bility of private universities and further enhances the greatness of
Brown University. The future looks bright and augers well for both
the Medical School Program and Brown.

As a Trustee Emeritus, I will give my loyal and undying support to
Brown University.

Sincerely,

Frank M. Yatsu, M.D.

FMY/jmg

Frank M. Yatsu

English and American Literature, 1955

Trustee, 1969 – 1974

January 20, 1992

Mr. Henry D. Sharpe, Jr.
Secretary to the Corporation
Brown University
Providence, Rhode Island 02912

Dear Henry:

I am happy to respond to your letter of January 17, 1992, knowing that at Brown, resignations from the Board are really promotions rather than withdrawals. Now I join the ranks of Brown's senior kibitzers, those who enjoy all the perks of Board membership without any of the responsibilities. For this reason, I look forward to standing shoulder to shoulder with all of you as before but with the added pleasure of being able to second guess you all the way.

My best to you and Brown. My years on this Board have been among the most rewarding and stimulating of my career. Thank you for having me.

Sincerely Yours,

Michael P. Gross

———

Michael P. Gross
International Studies, 1964
Trustee, 1986 – 1992

WENDY J. STROTHMAN
SECRETARY
BROWN UNIVERSITY CORPORATION   APRIL 6, 1999
BOX 1887
PROVIDENCE, RHODE ISLAND 02912

DEAR WENDY,

    THE FOLLOWING DOGGEREL MUST SERVE TO EXPRESS MY SENTIMENTS AND ACCOMPLISH ITS ONEROUS FUNCTION:

WITH LEADEN HEART AND SPIRITS LOW
I TAKE MY PEN IN HAND,
POISED TO WRITE THE DREADED WORDS
THAT TRADITION DOTH DEMAND.

THE ACT ITSELF DENIES THE GRIEF,
FOR THE CARING LINGERS ON,
LET'S FACE IT, THERE'S JUST NO RELIEF
FOR SOON I SHALL BE GONE.

BUT WAIT, THERE'S HOPE, THE DOOR'S AJAR
AND A LIGHT JUST GLIMMERS THROUGH
THERE IS SOME JOY, THERE APPEARS A WAY
TO REMAIN FOREVER TRUE.

AS I SHED MY ROLE, CAN I SOOTHE MY SOUL
KNOWING NOTHING FOREVER LASTS?
YES, THE LATIN TONGUE DEFINES MY FATE,
"TRUSTEE EMERITUS".

WHEN TIME AND MILES MAKE WIDE THE GULF
AND WE LOOK FROM A DISTANT SHORE
THERE SHINES A BEACON, LET'S CALL IT LOVE
THAT LINKS US FOREVER MORE.

FOR THE BROWN THAT WE KNOW AND THE BROWN THAT IS NEW
OUR SPIRITS ARE FILLED WITH PRIDE
AND AS OTHERS DWELL WHERE ONCE WE STOOD
OUR GHOSTS WILL THERE RESIDE

SO HERE IS MY MISSIVE, ITS MESSAGE CLEAR
WITH WORDS THAT APPEAR MOST BENIGN
BUT THEY MASK THE EMOTION THAT ROILS WITHIN
WHEN, ALAS, I MUST WRITE " I RESIGN"

ROBERT P. SANCHEZ
CLASS OF 1958

Robert P. Sanchez

English Literature, 1958

Trustee, 1993 – 1999

I am finding it increasingly difficult, as my term
expires, to find the words with which to resign.

—BARBARA MOSBACHER SMULLYAN

———

English, 1945
Trustee, 1969 – 1974

W. DUNCAN MacMILLAN II

SOCIIS CURATORIBUS MINISTRIS

SALUTATIONES

HAC MEA TERTIA EPISTULA AD MUNERA DEPONENDA VOBIS
SCRIPTA ITERABO ID QUOD VOBIS ANTEA ASSEVERAVI, SCILICET
NATURAM UNIVERSITATIS BRUNENSIS PERPETUO VI ET OPIBUS
MAGNOPERE AUGESCERE.   ADHUC AB ANNIS QUINQUENGENARIIS
SEXAGENARIISQUE SEX PRAESIDES PERMULTOS MINISTROS
PROFESSORES STUDENTES ADIUTORES COGNOVI, ATTAMEN
UNIVERSITAS NOSTRA HOC TEMPORE OMNIMODIS EST
PRAESTANTISSIMA.   LICET ME EX ANTERIORE PORTA EIECTAS,
POSTERIORE REVERTAR.

W. Duncan MacMillan II
to Fellows, Trustees and Officials
Greetings.

With this third letter of resignation I have written to you I shall repeat
what I stated to you earlier, namely that Brown University continues to
increase greatly both in strength and in resources. From the 50's and
60's to the present I have come to know six presidents, many administrators,
professors, students, staff members, and yet our university is at this time
in every way most excellent. You may push me out the front door, but I will
return through the back door.

Post-it™ brand fax transmittal memo 7671 # of pages ▶ 1

To _Susan J. Brown_	From _W. F. Wyatt Jr._
Co.	Co. _Classics Dept._
Dept.	Phone #
Fax # _7737_	Fax # _7484_

W. Duncan MacMillan II

Classics, 1953

Honorary Doctor of Laws, 1993

Trustee, 1974 – 1979, 1980 – 1985, 1988 – 1994, 1995 – 2001

HALE AND DORR
COUNSELLORS AT LAW

AREA CODE 617 HUBBARD 2-3300

CABLE ADDRESS "HAFIS"

October 11, 1963

John Nicholas Brown, Esq.
Secretary, Brown University
Providence 12, Rhode Island

Dear Mr. Brown:

I thank you for your letter with the news that
I have been elected to membership in that exclusive club
known as the Trustees Emeriti of Brown. That is an honor
to which the handsome and distinguished gentlemen on the
other side of the aisle can never look forward -- when
one of them leaves us usually it is to strum a golden
harp in company that some of us might find a bit dull.

I have been fortunate indeed to have been a
member of this body over the most important decade in the
history of Brown. It has been a happy ship with a skill-
ful captain who has the confidence and affection of all
the crew.

I submit herewith my resignation as a Trustee,
happy in the knowledge that he and his crew will bring
us through the next decade with flying colors.

Yours sincerely,

Daniel L. Brown

Daniel L. Brown

Bachelor of Arts, 1912

Honorary Doctor of Laws, 1962

Trustee, 1952 – 1959, 1960 – 1963

I would love to be the first trustee who refuses
to resign, but I guess I cannot do that.

—ALAN G. HASSENFELD

———

Trustee, 1990 – 1996, 2020 – 2026

President Howard R. Swearer inauguration, Sayles Hall, 1977

One Last Thing
Before I Go . . .

I want to take this chance to offer one parting
thought. I hope that the Corporation will seek a
wide ranging and diverse mix of backgrounds and
viewpoints in its future membership. It is through the
fires of divergence, not the comforts of homogeneity,
that this storied institution shines the brightest.

—THOMAS E. ROTHMAN

———

English and American Literature, 1976
Trustee, 2009 – 2015

May 2011

Dear Don,

To this day I aspire to the level of cultural competency that Maurice Glicksman, the University Provost, expressed to us, the graduating seniors in 1983:

> "I hope that we have helped you to recognize others as the individual human beings they are. Our world depends for its survival on our living together and understanding each other as individuals and as people with different cultures and different sets of goals. We must move from the judgment of others by our own standards, past the toleration of difference, to the support of diverse views and goals."

Some have suggested that there is a correlation between racism and classism. In part that is true. However, education, wealth, technology, and even the Presidency of the United States, does not shield you from racism. In fact, it becomes more subtle and insipid. We and, more tragically, our children still have to deal with it. That is why it is so important for our schools to educate all children on the challenges and the advantages of diversity in our community. Without the vision, attention, and commitment of those responsible for our schools' policies and priorities those efforts will take longer to be successful or not succeed at all. At Brown, it is the responsibility of the Corporation to adopt and promote those policies and priorities. It has been 50 years since women and men, Jews and Christians, Blacks and whites, rode together in support of equality. Our Board, in its own way, should honor those efforts by continuing to make diversity a priority.

We have hired exceptional faculty of diverse backgrounds, but we cannot stop, we cannot even rest. There is enormous competition for all of our outstanding faculty, and we have to work incessantly to retain them and hire more of them.

We have an extraordinary student body representing an incredible spectrum of religions, ethnicities, and sexual preferences. Again, as with faculty, we cannot let up. We need to examine our graduation rates for African American and Hispanic students and work to get them on par with the non-Hispanic white graduation rate. We must analyze how many students of color write Cap Stones, graduate Phi Beta Kappa or Cum Laude, or pursue dual concentrations. And then prospectively, examine where they go to graduate school. Are they going to the top graduate schools? How do their statistics compare to those of their white colleagues? We need to revise our University Mission Statement and address diversity. We must collect all mission statements throughout the University, including that for the Third World Center that currently refers to 'Third World Students" and "Third World people at Brown University." We must acknowledge that if it takes three paragraphs to explain the name "Third World Center," as one senior administrator reported, then it does not reflect the experience of a prospective 18-year-old. If we are to matriculate the best students of color, let us speak their language, let us speak to their experiences. The programs at the TWC are fantastic and must continue, but they need to be broadened to help all students learn from each other. And of course, our financial aid packages must stay competitive for students of color who are also being sought out by our sister schools.

As a Corporation we have an obligation to follow up on all aspects of the Plan for Academic Enrichment, including its diversity goals. As a University we are aspiring to a greater global presence. We strive to prepare our students to work in a global environment. As quoted on one of the walls of the Library, John D. Rockefeller said, "I believe that every right implies a responsibility; every opportunity an obligation." We have a responsibility and opportunity to prepare our students to feel comfortable among different cultures and religions, as they enter an ever increasingly diverse world.

The 2010 Census report noted Hispanics contributed to more than half of the growth in the US population. The Hispanic population grew to 55.5 million in 2010, up from 35.3 million in 2000, a 43% increase. Hispanics now account for one in every four people in the United States under the age of 18. The population that identified itself as white alone grew by only 5.7%. Those identifying as Black or African American alone grew by 12.3%, Asian alone grew by 43%. Nearly 92% of our nation's population growth of 25.1 million over the past decade was among self-identified minorities, including people of mixed races. These statistics cannot be ignored. Diversity is part of who we are as a nation and, to serve our students, needs to be part of who we are as an academic community.

It is heartfelt when I say it was an honor to be the first Hispanic woman alumna trustee. It has been an enormous responsibility and one that I hope I fulfilled with integrity befitting my alma mater. I hope many more women and many more men and women of color also have the honor to serve on the Corporation.

It is with a heavy heart that I resign from the Corporation. While my engagement with the Brown Corporation is ended, my commitment to remain Ever True to Brown is unwavering.

Warm personal regards,

Carmen

———

Carmen M. Rodriguez
Organizational Behavior Management, 1983
Trustee, 2005 – 2011

DEPARTMENT OF ENGLISH

SYRACUSE, NEW YORK 13210
315/423-2173/74

JEAN E. HOWARD (MRS. JAMES BAKER)

May 16, 1981

Judge Alfred H. Joslin
Secretary of the Corporation
University Hall
Brown University
Providence, Rhode Island 02912

Dear Judge Joslin:

I hate to resign from the Corporation, but I will, realizing that there are many others waiting for the opportunity to serve Brown as a Trustee and knowing that my experience on the Board has only strengthened my ties to an institution that I love very dearly. There are, I am sure, many ways to serve Brown once the days of active trusteeship are over.

I am not sure what I will miss most--probably Hank Sharpe's wonderful reports. As one who spends her professional life teaching English, I think I have taken special delight in my fellow trustee's creative manipulation of the Mother Tongue. I shall miss, on October, February, and May afternoons, being exhorted, while biting the bullet, to take the bull by the horns and run with it. I am glad to have been thus admonished.

As I leave the Board, my deepest feelings are of gratitude. I am grateful for the exhilerating college experience Brown gave to me over a decade ago. I am grateful for the unique experience of serving Brown as a Trustee and for the generous way so many of you in this room made me feel welcome when I was new to the Corporation and its ways. I am grateful that, largely through your efforts, places like Brown are still flourishing in the 1980's. And since it is now time for me to pack my gear and move on, I would like to say two things. First, I hope there will always be a place on this Board for the young and the inexperienced, as well as for more seasoned heads. What we add to your deliberations is not for me to say; what we take from them is incalcuably valuable. There is no surer way to create a cadre of life-long Brown devotees. Second, I hope there will always be a place in this room for discussion of educational policy and institutional values. We raise money and balance budgets because we absolutely must if Brown is to survive. But Brown must survive so that students and faculty--the heart of this place--can pursue truth in freedom and show us how to shape a more just future. To forget, because pragmatic problems are so pressing, the larger cause we serve is to risk making choices that will harm what we cherish.

Resignation letters should be brief. I threaten to be as long-winded as Polonius. In October, February, and May I shall think of you all and of Brown with deep affection.

Sincerely,

Jean E. Howard

Jean E. Howard

English and American Literature, 1970

Honorary Doctor of Humane Letters, 2016

Trustee, 1974 – 1981

JOHN B. HENDERSON

February 8, 1990

Mr. Henry D. Sharpe, Jr.
Secretary of the Corporation
Brown University
Box 1887
Providence, RI   02912

Dear Henry:

With regret, I submit my resignation effective
June 30.

Echoing the refrain I have heard from so many others,
I leave the Brown Corporation with a deep sense of
the privilege it has been to serve with such a
stimulating and delightful group dedicated to
increasing the excellence of a university we all
cherish. It has been a special pleasure to have had
the chance to serve as a Trustee at a time in my
career when I have not had to rob Peter to pay Paul.
I have had enough time for committee assignments and
have therefore been able to enjoy them doubly.

The Brown to which from the countryside I came half a
century ago was a charming, if somewhat parochial,
regional college. But under Henry Merritt Wriston it
was on the move. Today's Brown has achieved an
almost magical and, from the point of view of the
undergraduates at least, joyful greatness. Mr.
Wriston, I suspect, would be more delighted than
surprised if he could see what he and his successors
have wrought.

I have had the pleasure and privilege of seeing Brown
come to new heights of excellence under Howard
Swearer. Now we turn to President Gregorian for the
leadership required to maintain and enrich the very
special excellence which is Brown. So far as I know,
the Corporation did not promise Greg a rose garden.
Simply a great school with great challenges. In that
context, I leave you with one suggestion.

The Corporation has been doing a fine job in dealing
with each discreet challenge Brown faces, including
funding. But we don't walk on water. To my chagrin,
I have heard Greg say that he also doesn't. Absent
that facility, it seems to me that some very serious
choices must be made in this decade to prevent Brown
from sliding imperceptibly but inexorably from
excellence toward mediocrity. I suggest that the
Corporation establish a group to focus on those hard
choices. Brown cannot do it all and have it all.
But the right choices, whatever they are, will bring
down the wrath of vested interests. The more the
Corporation takes the hits for hard choices, or at
least shares them with the President, the better Greg
will be able to lead this delightful University to
new heights.

                    Sincerely,

JBH:sg

John B. Henderson
English, 1946
Trustee, 1984 – 1990

May 15, 2015

Dear Don,

It is my bittersweet duty to tender my resignation as a member of the Corporation effective June 30, 2015. It has been a tremendous honor to serve Brown these last six years equally divided under the extraordinary leadership of President Ruth Simmons and President Christina Paxson. It has been particularly significant to me that I arrived with the first young trustee, Lauren Kolodny, followed by Eric Rodriguez and Alison Cohen. All three of these young people have shown me the result of the superb education of younger generations at Brown and I am proud to have served by their side. I greatly look forward to continuing to follow their futures. I have learned about trustee leadership from Tom Tisch, Jerome Vascellaro, Alison Ressler, and Nancy Neff and was proud to serve as her Vice Chair on Campus Life. I was also so grateful for the early tutelage of Tony Ittleson and Marty Granoff . . . Tony should teach a course entitled "Trustee 101"!!! Having played as many leaders as I have in my work as an actress, I continuously marveled in observing the extraordinary women and men on the faculty and the staff meet the demands of running this tremendous institution. As wistful as I am that I am coming to the end of my time as a trustee, I am very clear that I will continue to focus my attention on the performing and theater arts programs. I have an abiding passion that Brown continue to have an astounding position in the arts and look forward to the creation of even more programs and the construction of more state-of-the-art venues for live performance. A great university, like a great nation, deserves the best in the arts. Brown should rightly continue to be a great university that has stupendous programs in the arts and I will continue to devote the rest of my life to this endeavor. I walked onto this campus 40 rainy springs ago for the first time as a high school student. Little did I know that this university would have such a profound effect on my life and on the life of my family. I am eternally grateful for my time on the Corporation and shall always remain ever true to Brown.

Kate Burton

———

Kate Burton
History and Russian Studies, 1979
Honorary Doctor of Fine Arts, 2007
Trustee, 2009 – 2015, 2019 – 2022

The Lindemann Performing Arts Center, designed by Joshua Ramus/REX and located at the heart of Brown University's campus, was dedicated October 20, 2023.

May 26, 2004

Dear Wendy,

Today brings to a close my second six-year term as a member of the Brown Corporation, but a period of close to twenty years of continuous service. Throughout my emeritus period from '91 to '98, I continued to serve as Chairman of the Committee on Facilities and Design.

My passion has been for the physical fabric of Brown in this neighborhood where I was born and grew up. My lifelong interest in architecture and urbanism has made it a privilege to serve and to learn. Campus design, especially at Brown, is really urban design.

The physical fabric of Brown engages two different parts of our responsibility and mentality as trustees. The first is the physical plant's essence as a container made up of a few thousand interior spaces, playing fields, and gathering places in which the educational and research mission is carried out. For this physical endowment, at least equivalent in value to our fiscal one, there is an endless challenge of growth, adaptation, and utilization. At the other side of our Brown conscience comes the aesthetic and environmental aspects of the campus and of its enormous meaning to students, the faculty, the local community, and to the collective memory of alumni spread across the country and the world. Brown has an unusual sense of spirit and place. Our 120-acre architectural vineyard on this hill, dynamic but also fragile, must be tended to first by its full-time stewards and their advisors, but its long-term oversight must remain a primary responsibility of the trustees of the University.

Beyond my own family and work, there is no activity that I have given more to than to Brown. I see the University in a new era of great good will and positive sentiment after a period of some drift. This new spirit is felt on campus and across the country within our constituency. I wish Ruth Simmons and the Corporation the best in carrying on our great mission, now two-and-a-half centuries old.

Respectfully,

Vincent Buonanno

—

Vincent J. Buonanno
Italian, 1966
Trustee, 1985 – 1991, 1998 – 2004

We stand together in a common cause, periodically feeling helpless as a great university searches for new directions and consolidates its acknowledged strengths.

—PAUL H. JOHNSON

————

International Relations, 1958
Trustee, 1972 – 1977

May 2017

Dear Don,

As you've heard from nearly everyone who has written you a letter since you took this highly paid job, I write to you begrudgingly and with sadness given that it marks the end of my tenure on this fantastic and esteemed Board. Unless, of course, you choose to reject this letter for which I'm happy to compensate you.

This chapter of my life began in 2003, while I was still working in the Pentagon and invited some folks from the Brown Medical School down to meet with me and some colleagues in DoD and VA who focused on future technologies regarding wounded soldiers. My purpose was not hidden: this was soon after 9/11 and I wanted to make sure that Brown, the institution I love, helped in the multi-generation battle of arms and ideas. Brown isn't Hopkins or MIT—we aren't going to design bombs or next generation ammunition. But, I thought, we could help in other ways, some of which Brown was already doing, and some new. Long story short, Brown received a number of important grants over the next several years focused principally on PTSD, and limb lengthening, an important issue for soldiers returning home without full arms and legs.

That led, over time, to my service on the Medical School Committee for a number of years and then on this Corporation.

Serving on this Corporation has been a great honor and a fantastic learning adventure. I will hold fast the many lessons that I have learned from the people I have met, from the Administration to the faculty to the students and, of course, the dedicated members of the Corporation.

And, I hope, in some small ways, I made a difference, for that is why we are all here. I enjoyed every aspect of my service—from serving on Campus Life, on the Brown Coal Divest Task Force, on a number of governance task forces, on the Med School Committee, and, most recently, on the Audit Committee: the best Corporation Committee.

Audit, I like to think, has your back. Its charter is to try to keep us all out of trouble, off the front pages, and to probe and poke to see if things are as they seem to be. For us as trustees and fellows, risk is something we should have front and center in our minds and after having served on the Audit Committee for a number of years, I feel confident that while we must all remain vigilant, our senior Administration leaders do an excellent job assessing risk and finding ways to mitigate such risks. We are in very good hands.

If I can leave you with one thought for Brown, it is this: Academic freedom and open discourse must stand above all other ideals, agendas, and blowing winds. It needs to be, alongside excellence, what defines Brown. We can't just pay lip service to the free exchange of ideas: we as a Corporation need to ensure it and hold the institution we love accountable for it. Our campus must be a place where all students are willing to engage in discussion and dialogue, not just those with a particular political persuasion. We as a Corporation should push to ensure that ideological diversity, along with all other types of diversity, is a Brown hallmark.

Telling students what should be important to them, and what they should think, is a slippery slope. If students are told that their viewpoint, political ideology, or conception of social justice is wrong, or are only taught that one ideology is right, will they voice their opinion and engage in active dialogue? Will they be the type of citizen we hope to help educate?

The corollary is a deep and abiding emphasis on academic excellence. I know Chris is highly focused on this and, to her credit, has been championing the primary importance for Brown to be and be seen as focused on academic excellence.

Other than supporting our President—the greatest University president in the country—I view the primary task of this Board to take active steps to make sure that academic and intellectual freedom still shines at Brown. It is my greatest hope for Brown, and my greatest fear.

With respect to you, Don, and to you, Chris, and your amazing team, and to each member of the Corporation.

Thank you.

Ever True,

Steven Price '84

_____

Steven Price
History, 1984
Trustee, 2011 – 2017

May 22, 2003

Wendy Strothman
Secretary
The Corporation Brown University
P. O. Box 1887
Providence, RI 02912

Dear Wendy:

As I promised I would—I am submitting my resignation as a Trustee of the University and member of Brown's Corporation. Seven years—with three Chancellors, five Presidents (or acting Presidents), more Provosts (or acting Provosts) than I can recall—a start in Providence and six years in London, have slipped by too quickly.

It is unlikely that I will ever be asked to hold a position that means more to me. I will always value the time I have spent with the exceptional people I have worked with at Brown. Ruth Simmons is the most exceptional of all—and I am disappointed to be leaving the Corporation as she begins to implement so many initiatives that will permit her to realize her vision for the University.

Although I do have unreserved admiration for Ruth, and respect for the team she has recruited, I do want to suggest to all of you who remain on the Corporation that it is critical that you be certain to express concerns that you may have and to challenge initiatives you may question. The Corporation constitutes the collective memory of the University and provides essential continuity as administrations come and go. I think in many ways Nancy Buc has been a model to us in challenging, questioning—and at times startling—but always energizing—our discussions. I wish more Corporation members did this.

I will always do what I can for Brown. I look forward to working with you and other members of the Corporation in any way that can be helpful.

Sincerely,

J. Scott Burns, Jr.
English and American Literature, 1969
Trustee, 1996 – 2003

JOSEPH L. DOWLING, JR., M.D.

October 10, 1984

Mrs. Ruth B. Ekstrom
Secretary of the Corporation
Brown University
Providence, RI 02912

Dear Ruth:

As Howard once said (and I think he got this from Alva Way), "today's peacock
is tomorrow's feather duster"; and so, with regret, I hereby submit my resignation
as a Trustee effective June 30, 1985.

However, since a peacock who sits on his feathers is just another turkey, I
take this occasion to offer a brief but not so modest assessment of these past
four years.

First, I have appreciated the opportunity to observe the dedication and
competence consistently demonstrated by the leadership of our University.
Howard Swearer and Dick Salomon are a remarkable team. Under their leadership,
the future of Brown is bright.

The years of my term have been eventful. The successful conclusion of the
Campaign for Brown, the Athletic Center, the Geo-Chemistry Building and other
new construction, the Sports Foundation, the new medical education curriculum
and the computerization of the University are a few of the accomplishments
which will be landmarks in the history of Brown. I have been privileged to
participate through the Corporation Committee on Athletics, the Student Life
Committee, the Medical Affairs Committee, the Nominating Committee and the
subcommittees on Student Health, the new Student Center, and University Patent
Policy.

I leave with one suggestion. Service as a trustee is a special honor and
responsibility. Under the present structure of three meetings a year, it is
often a considerable time before a new trustee feels comfortable in his role.
Perhaps, an informal, primarily social, retreat for a day or two after the
fall meeting to enable the new and old trustees to know each other would effect
a more productive and satisfying trusteeship.

Finally I would like to express my sincere thanks to my fellow corporation
members, Howard and his staff, and the many others who have made these years
so memorable and enjoyable.

Sincerely,

Joe Dowling

Joseph L. Dowling, Jr., M.D.

JLD:bfl

Joseph L. Dowling, Jr.

Biology, 1947

Trustee, 1980 – 1985

FEB 7 1986

MICHAEL-WALTERS INDUSTRIES, INC.

Margaret C. Michael, President/Chairman of the Board

February 3, 1986

Mrs. Ruth B. Ekstrom, Secretary
Brown University Board of Trustees
Providence, Rhode Island 02912

Dear Ruth, and Fellow Board Members:

Today I would like to address THE CHAIR.

Not the tactful, distinguished, Chairman of our Board of Trustees ...
nor the handsome, unparalleled President of our University and Fellows ...

not even the gracious Chairman of IBM nor the Illustrious Chairs of a myriad
of varied and sundry Industrial, Civic, and Private Boards represented in
this verdantly venerated room.

Rather, I would address THE CHAIR in which you are sitting.

To those new to this experience: don't despair. You are not the only one
who doesn't fit. Your chair may actually be among the most uniquely shaped
chairs in the Nation.

At Brown we believe in being first in everything.

However, as my own short years of adjustment are coming to an end, I find
that one of us - either THE CHAIR or I - has become better padded. My
position has been buffered by the memorable, educational, challenging, and
all-around fascinating association with stimulating, generous, brilliant, warm,
friendly, devoted Alumni.

It is with gratitude and regret, therefore, that I tender my resignation
effective June 30, 1986, and look forward to returning ... more experienced,
wiser, and more properly suited and seated in THE CHAIR of Trustee Emeriti.

Sincerely,

"Reggie"

Margaret Conant Michael '51

P.S. Wishing to leave something Concrete Behind, I have attached herewith
a relatively modest check to purchase personalized pillows for future
Corporation sit-ins. However, should the fund-raising powers find
there are more pressing priorities, I reluctantly release the designated
monies for loftier, though perhpas none more welcome, purposes.

Margaret Conant Michael

English Literature, 1951

Trustee, 1981 – 1986

May 20, 1999

Ms. Wendy J. Strothman,
Secretary of the Corporation Brown University,
Providence, RI 02912

Dear Wendy:

I started this letter by writing,

> "Almost 60 years of active connection with Brown are drawing to a close. The Secretary's call for yet one more (and final) 'Resignation Letter' fills me with an eerie sense of wistfulness . . . "

But even before I could complete this nostalgic sentence, technology stepped in to interrupt it with an unexpected question, which might be far more germane than I had expected. It begged an answer on a subject that I myself would never have been bold enough to write about, had I not first been prompted.

The technological interruption came from my computer. When I started to write " . . . fills me with an eerie <u>wistfulness</u>," its spell-checker stopped me to ask if I hadn't really meant, " . . . fills me with a sense of <u>wastefulness</u>."

Well, surely a lifetime at Brown has not been <u>wasted</u>, for it is an undeniable honor and satisfaction to feel that one has been able to contribute even a little bit to Brown's fantastic progress during this period. And it is especially rewarding to realize that Brown's progress is now also seen by the whole world as a growing and valuable contribution to learning and civilization.

But I am suddenly moved by this chance juxtaposition of "wistfulness" and "wastefulness." An embryo in the back of my mind has been unexpectedly stirred.

It is impossible not to look back at the relatively simple but sophisticated Brown of Wriston that we knew as undergraduates in the 1940s without drawing comparisons with today that shake the soul.

> The prodigious variety of course offerings and sports,
> The diminished relationship between instructional salaries and the overall budget,
> The number of Deans, and special advisors,

The elaborateness, albeit the undeniable beauty, of our facilities,

The number of committees needed to assure Brown's accreditation,

The hours spent in those committees and other "reviews" that are not spent teaching,

The number of security officers and their required procedures and equipment,

The number and elaborateness of invitations, designed, mailed, and having to be replied to, to maintain a yearlong comet's tail of dazzling "events" and structure each resplendent Commencement,

and, of course,

The superb yet numerous Development Staff that powers it all, so successfully.

Such comparisons certainly trace a dilemma, an infection of modern society. On one hand we have ordained that all such elaborations (and many, many others not cited), are now considered "necessary" for "progress" and "success," for, it is said, the world is admittedly complex, changing rapidly, and competition is highly charged. On the other, that condition raises an appropriate question: How do we retain the ability to honestly assess those minimum devotions, talents, and disciplines that are <u>necessary</u> to produce an educated person, and eschew all that is a confusing, burdensome excess?

As I leave, I am haunted by this question my dumb computer has asked, almost as if it had read my mind. Should I have opened my letter, saying,

> "The Secretary's call for . . . [a] 'Retirement Letter' fills me with an eerie sense of <u>wastefulness</u> . . . ?"

Now that I am prompted, on reflection, maybe I <u>should</u> have, for after all, I must humbly admit that even my <u>own</u> actions over the years in this body have helped to frame the dilemma.

Now that we are beginning a promising and careful exploration of our future, out of respect, I can only bequeath to you that haunting <u>question</u> in trust that we will all bear it constantly in mind as the new plans go forward.

The virtues of a humbler, simpler life are hard to find in modern times. Some may even say they are passé, but I still suspect they still have much relevance toward building what our Charter calls men and women, " . . . of Usefulness and Reputation." And these virtues, alas, are most poignantly, most effectively, taught by <u>example</u>.

How well <u>are</u> we teaching <u>that</u> course?

Yours, with an Effusion of Affection, Loyalty, and Respect, and, in the end,

Truly, a Heartfelt Wistfulness,

Henry D. Sharpe, Jr.

─────

Henry D. Sharpe, Jr.
Economics, 1945
Honorary Doctor of Laws, 1970
Vice Chancellor, 1985 – 1988
Secretary, 1988 – 1998
Trustee, 1954 – 1961, 1964 – 1969, 1972 – 1978, 1979 – 1982, 1985 – 1988
Fellow, 1982 – 1985, 1988 – 1999

Brown University President Christina H. Paxson (right)
and former President Ruth J. Simmons (left), 2012

One final bit of advice:
If your goals for Brown don't scare you,
they are not sufficiently high.

—STEVEN ROBERT

————

Political Science, 1962
Honorary Doctor of Humane Letters, 2004
Vice Chancellor, 1997 – 1998
Chancellor, 1998 – 2007
Trustee, 1984 – 1990, 1991 – 1994, 1997 – 2007
Fellow, 1994 – 1997, 2007 – 2012

". . . being located in the center of New England, and with One of the most liberal Charters that has ever been granted to warrant and secure a Fair and generous equality to be extended to every Religious Sect, which I do most sincerely recommend to every Branch in the Government of said College . . ."

———

John Brown
Petitioner of The College
Honorary Master of Arts, 1773
Treasurer, 1775 – 1796
Trustee, 1775 – 1803

239
(c)

Providence September 6. 1803
Tuesday Morning

Gentlemen

Finding the State of my Health, fast declin[ing]
which together with my Inactivity of Body, and long cont[inued]
Lameness, has, and will continue to render me a useless [member]
of the Corporation, and wishing as I do, that some one who [may]
have it in his power, as well as Inclination, to promote the welfare [of the Institution]
should be elected in my place, I now take this early Oppor[tunity to]
Resign my seat in the Corporation, desiring that it may be [done]
as Your Wisdom shall direct, during the present annual [meeting]

In small States like ours, where the Legi[slature]
gives but little pecuniary aid, to found Literary Institutions, [and support]
them, there remains of course, greater exertions for the well [wishers of]
Individuals to bring to maturity such seats of Learning, a[nd enable]
our College to become. But when we Consider that 33 Years [have]
passed since the Foundations of our College Edifice were laid [the pro]
gress of the Institution has not been very inconsiderable, [although we]
have attended impediments during that time has much impeded the [Institu]
for increase of Students The great Revolutionary W[ar by which]
we obtaind our Independence, was a great Stagnation [to the Insti]
tution, the College Edifice having been taken and apply'd to th[e use of an]
Hospital, and for Barracking the Troops, for nearly one Sixth [of the]
whole time from its foundation to this day. This circumstan[ces]
are certainly sufficient motives to induce us to Hope, & Expect [that the]
Patrons and Promoters of Literature, to step forward and [support]
the College under Your directions; Being located in the [State of New]
England, and with One of the most Liberal Charters t[hat ever was]
been granted to warrant and secure a fair and generou[s support]
be extended to every Religious Sect, which I do most si[ncerely]
P. T[illinghast]

The President & Corporation
of Rhode Island College

Brown University Coat of Arms, Wayland Arch, 2023

Lives of Usefulness and Reputation

. . . we are the current guardians of Brown's character, its values, its culture, and its mission to educate and prepare students to discharge the offices of life with usefulness and reputation.

—JEROME C. VASCELLARO

———

Engineering, 1974
Honorary Doctor of Humane Letters, 2024
Vice Chancellor, 2007 – 2016
Trustee, 1999 – 2005, 2007 – 2016
Fellow, 2016 – 2021

May 20, 1992

Mr. Henry D. Sharpe Jr.
Box 1887 Brown University
Providence, RI 02912

Dear Henry and My Fellow Humans of the Brown Corporation,

Some of the most interesting and enjoyable aspects of my life have been related to my involvement with Brown University, first as a student,and subsequently as an alumnus, a Trustee and a Fellow. As a student, I was enriched by the wise guidance of Presidents Wriston and Keeney. As a Fellow I have been privileged to serve under the visionary leadership of Presidents Swearer and Gregorian. What a glorious heritage!

During my 39-year relationship with Brown I have witnessed the academic growth of the University to unparalleled heights of popularity, notoriety and esteem in virtually all sectors of our national community.

I have seen the political issues of minorities go through several cycles, spiralling upward toward the pluralist ideal. I have debated in this room with my good friend, Mike Trotter - the issue of the value and timeliness of the pluralist ideal. It would appear on the surface that the White Southerner was advocating integration and the African-American Southerner was purporting segregation. The tone was that of a healthy family argument and we know that the issue was much more complex and profound than just depicted. Witnessing the maturation and development of this great institution toward achieving the highest ideals,as regards issues of race, gender, and ethnicity, has been deeply gratifying. Significant challenges in this sphere remain before us and I am confident that Brown will meet them.

For 20 years there has been the opportunity to observe continued growth, development and new levels of major achievements in the program of medical education, now known as the medical school. To my esteemed colleague and friend, Dick Solomon, not to worry, the medical school will remain an asset to the University and not dishevel its academic ecological balance.

It is intriguing to observe, to analyze and to describe the culture of institutions. This is a way of personifying an institution. Having studied Brown University for almost 40 years, I would personify it as a noble, humane, powerful, innovative, intelligent, wise institution. We are, indeed, very fortunate to be affiliated.

An institution is a total of the individuals that comprise it. I would like to express my thanks for the opportunity of having thoroughly enjoyed Brown students, faculty, administrators, alumni, trustees, fellows, and auxiliary staff over the last 39 years.

I will close by thanking this great University for the contribution it made to my education as an undergraduate and subsequently for further educating me and enriching my life as an adult.

My apologies for the length of this letter, but this is important and I only get one shot.

Be well,

Augustus A. White III, M.D.

Augustus A. White III

Psychology, 1957

Honorary Doctor of Medical Science, 1997

Trustee, 1971 – 1976

Fellow, 1981 – 1992

ARTEMIS A.W. JOUKOWSKY
Chancellor Emeritus

BROWN UNIVERSITY
BOX 1964 PROVIDENCE, RHODE ISLAND 02912
TEL. 401-863-1756 · FAX. 401-272-9594

May 18, 2009

Donald C. Hood
Secretary of the Corporation
Brown University
Box 1887
Providence, RI 02912

Dear Secretary of the Corporation,

I have listened to the reading of letters of resignation written by a myriad of wonderful Trustees and Fellows and twisted in my seat to hear sincere expressions of deep emotion and sadness accompanied at times with bittersweet humor which provided that special temporary relief . I clearly remember how often I became engrossed and experienced a meditative uneasiness with the thought that one day I would write such a letter myself.

Well, here I am composing and promising myself that my letter would be brief and that I would not torture the listeners with my own feelings and emotions. Make them laugh and enjoy your letter, I mused. Express and tell them all of the close to lifetime love for dear old Brown.

I am in my 24th year as a member of the Corporation. During this lengthy passage of time, it became clear to me, as I am sure it has to you, that there is a meaning to a place—a meaning that can be made up of one's friends and one's purpose in that place. I met the love of my life, Martha, as an undergraduate 55 years ago. This place provided us with the luxury to grow and spin our webs—a place that seems timeless. Intellectual stimulation, the beauty of New England, the heat and thrill of an athletic contest, , the warmth of many friendships, the majestic sweep of University Hall, the familiarity of the college green, the ringing of the belltower which provides the rhythm of each day. All these treasures connect us to the place that is Brown.

You already surmised that I am doing what I promised not to do but I am compelled to share my deep feelings of love and nostalgia as well as other thoughts about the future.

With all this in mind, I convey to each of you a very fond farewell. I feel solace that we will see each other again but, perhaps, not within this room. I will certainly miss the pleasure of your company.

This institution came into existence because a small visionary group of Rhode Islanders came together to found a college which has incrementally grown to become a major national and international university, an extraordinary attainment. As Trustees, you are now the keepers of the vision of the pioneers and leaders who have preceded us.

Leadership is not an abstract concept—a pro forma duty—it is rather a zestful active engagement of energy and imagination to make things work— things we believe in. This particularly becomes crystal clear when one thinks of the great leaders of the past and the present, with Chancellor Tom Tisch and our remarkable and singular President, Ruth Simmons.

Sincerely yours,

Artemis Joukowsky

Artemis A. W. Joukowsky, Jr.

Sociology, 1955

Honorary Doctor of Laws, 1985

Vice Chancellor, 1988 – 1997

Chancellor, 1997 – 1998

Trustee, 1985 – 1998

Fellow, 1998 – 2009

I remember asking at one of our first meetings, "Do we ever make decisions?" and I was told "No, you make recommendations." Well, I suppose after three hundred years you have to learn patience at Brown.

—PETER B. GREEN

———

Master of Arts, History, 1980
Trustee, 1997 – 2003

March 19, 2021

Richard Friedman
Secretary
Corporation Office
Brown University
Box 1887
Providence, RI 02912

Dear Mr. Friedman:

It has been an honor to serve as a New Alumni Trustee for the past two years. This unexpected journey began with nominations from people—some of whose names are still unknown to me—who saw a seat for me at this table that I hadn't yet envisioned for myself. Just five short months after earning my Ph.D., I took their faith in me as a challenge to continue the work I began as a student leader, to be willing to step into the unknown, and to bring my whole self to the role rather than try to fit a preconceived notion of who or what a trustee should be. As I moved further along in the process, and ultimately, once I learned my peers had elected me, I promised I would do all of those things to the best of my ability. And, if I have done all three in fulfilling my roles and responsibilities, my term will have been very well spent.

The unlikelihood of this two-time Duke graduate from "Bed-Stuy," Brooklyn, serving on this university's Board of Trustees is just one example of how Brown, at its best, has been a place of infinite possibility for me. It's where I enrolled in the second-ever cohort of a nascent doctoral program in Africana Studies and experienced its growth into one of the most well-respected in the nation in less than a decade. It's where people in high places are unafraid to reckon with the past—as with the pioneering "Slavery and Justice Report"—and to make changes and allocate resources necessary to improve the University as well as the lives of the people in its orbit. It's where students living openly in the fullness and complexity of their identities model love, understanding, and compassion for me and for so many others. It's where I've encountered people across backgrounds, affiliations, and generations who deeply believe the world can be a better place, and, most critically, that, when they work together, they have the power to make it so.

When I look at the many challenges facing universities, and, therefore, the rest of the nation and even the world, those qualities make Brown stand out—even among the most forward-thinking institutions—as a really special place. I am proud of how far the University has come, even as I recognize the unfinished and urgent work that lies ahead. I am grateful to have been welcomed into a community of trustees and fellows who are passionate about shaping Brown into a place that lives up to and exceeds its highest aspirations. So many have shown kindness and collegiality, sparked conversations, and expressed interest in where I've been, who I am, and who I want to become. I have faith that these connections will not end with my term, that new ones will arise, and that one day we will reunite—in person—on College Hill again.

It's fair to say my tenure as a Brown alumna has gotten off to a lofty start. But I know that this time on the Corporation has been just that—the beginning of a new chapter in my relationship to this beloved institution.

Ever true,

Amanda Boston

_____

Amanda T. Boston
Master of Arts, Africana Studies, 2016
Doctor of Philosophy, Africana Studies, 2018
Trustee, 2019 – 2021

May 12, 2017

Dr. Donald C. Hood, Secretary
Brown University, Corporation Office
Box 1887
Providence, RI 02912

Dear Don:

I regrettably am gripped now by writer's block, despite more than seven years to reflect on this inevitable letter. Given my heartfelt gratitude for my time on the Corporation and our years of collective good work, this note appropriately should be a short, cheerful, upbeat, sunny statement, both by tradition and by nature. Curiously, I find myself dwelling on death and dying. Where's the joy in that?!

You see, I started my term six months early because of the tragically premature loss of our friend, Joe Fernandez, my predecessor as BAA President, a genuinely good man of generous heart. During my term, I lost two dear brothers and both my beloved parents. Where's the joy in that?!

I just returned from Brazil and the Amazon where I saw first-hand the continuing destruction of habitat, species, water supplies, reserves for indigenous peoples, and the very air we breathe. A mile from my house in Florida, the world's third largest coral reef is dying. The Everglades are still under assault. Yards from my house on Cape Cod, the marshes (nurseries for countless food stocks) are clogged and dying. Canaries in the coal mine. The news from Washington grows more surreal every day, including the systematic destruction of principles and measures crafted, however imperfectly, to support health and security. Where's the joy in that?!

Before dark storm clouds and swarms of locusts converge on the Corporation Room, conjured by this line of unseemly thinking, I'll do my best to see the joy in that.

Two of the scientists I met in Brazil are talented, committed Brown faculty members. Like Joe Fernandez, my brothers, my parents, John Rowe Workman, Elmer Blistein, and Barrett Hazeltine, like so many other selfless Brown faculty members, countless committed staff, exceptional Brown Presidents, Provosts, Deans, conscientious Trustees, dedicated Fellows over the centuries, and, yes, Don, like YOU, like our friends in this room now, those two faculty members embody the combination of heart, brain, backbone, good will, and discipline that lead them to forge lives of usefulness and reputation.

Like so many others at Brown, they are working to create knowledge, to understand terribly complex interdependencies that carry profound risk and great opportunity. With others, they seek to craft practical, balanced solutions to seemingly impossible, intractable problems. They strive to make the world a better place. There's joy and hope in that.

The greatest joy in all of this, however, is the sincere gratitude I feel for the honor of serving with all of you, and for the great blessing of so many treasured and enduring friendships forged through our volunteer work for our great University. But for our work together, I would not have met most of you. My life has been enriched beyond measure by Brown. With so much talent in this room and throughout the Brown community, I have every confidence that Brown will continue to be a force for good long after I'm gone. The world needs that now more than ever.

So much for death and dying! I hereby submit my resignation as Trustee of Brown University effective June 30, 2017.

Sincerely,

George H. Billings, '72

———

George H. Billings
English and American Literature, 1972
Honorary Doctor of Humane Letters, 2021
Trustee, 2011 – 2017

Brown University President Christina H. Paxson leads the 2023
University ceremony.

May 9, 2016

Mr. Donald C. Hood Secretary, Brown Corporation
Brown University
Box 1887
Providence, R.I. 02912

Dear Don:

As the end of April approached, I began to think—or more accurately hope—that you had forgotten that my term was ending this June, and that I actually might be able to continue on the Corporation. Alas, a few days later the dreaded email arrived. I now prepare to join the others I have watched over the past several years say goodbye at the May Corporation meetings, and submit my resignation as of June 30th.

The last 8 years have been beyond special. When I joined the Corporation in the summer of 2008, I was encouraged to join the Budget and Finance Committee because it was "educational" and "fun" to decide where to spend the University's funds. So I did, only to receive my first package of Committee material in the fall of 2008 which detailed all the potential areas for cuts in the budget to deal with the economic recession. After this inauspicious beginning, I spent the next several years thoroughly enjoying my work on Audit (yes, Audit), Advancement, Committee on Fundraising, and my passion, Campus Life. I truly found my "home" on the Campus Life Committee and thank some wise, invisible "hand" for giving me the opportunity to do what I love most, which is to try to improve the lives of students on campus. I loved the issues we tackled, the increased student interactions we promoted, and the progress we made, most notably in athletics, dormitories, and career preparation. But, needless to say, there is still plenty of room for improvement!

I have had terrific partners along the way, and the great joy of working with old Brown friends while making wonderful new ones, including my "better half" on the Annual Fund, Todd Fisher. It has been one of the unexpected pleasures of this job to have befriended and worked side-by-side with such a fine and principled person. One of the other pleasures of co-chairing the Annual Fund has been participating in the full array of Reunion class gatherings, from the 5th to the 50th, and observing the differences in the character of the generations, but also the common love that exists for Brown and the profound appreciation for the University's impact on their lives.

My most satisfying experience on the Corporation was as a member of the Presidential Search Committee. Thanks to Tom's remarkable leadership, our large group representing all the constituencies of the University worked long hours, but with a common purpose, lack of ego, and good humor to arrive at a phenomenal choice. It has truly been an honor to serve under Chris and before her, Ruth, two extraordinary presidents and female leaders by whom I have been inspired, and exciting to work with what I believe is the strongest leadership team in the University's history, including Rick, Russell, Maude, Kevin, Pat, and many others.

It seems so fitting that my term on the Corporation ends with the conclusion of the chancellorship of one of my oldest friends, Tom, and coincides with the 40th reunion of our class. Tom and I met as 16-year-olds, shared Neusner's Reli Stu I and Beiser's Political Sci 116 together, have flown and driven to and from Corporation meetings together and, on Sunday, will march through the Van Wickle Gates together. Tom—you and Jerome have guided the Corporation with steady hands, thoughtful and wise minds, and passionate and compassionate hearts. Thank you.

I am moved that my last official act as a Trustee will be to present the Brown diploma to a young man—a first-gen—with whom I have been extremely close since his freshman year when he lost his mother. Brown has been a remarkable journey and community for him, and I have been able to experience again, on a very personal level, the life-changing impact of our University on its graduates. I can think of no finer way to honor my service to Brown than to celebrate his accomplishments at Commencement.

I want to wish Sam and his team the best of luck, and to thank all of you for your friendship, which has meant the world to me.

Sincerely,

Nancy Fuld Neff '76 P'06, P'14

———

Nancy Fuld Neff
Political Science, 1976
Trustee, 2008 – 2016

. . . we've covered everything from need-blind admissions to arming the police, from the need for better research facilities to the need for parking—and we've reached consensus every time. That consistent vision forged by diversity is something that makes this institution so strong.

—WENDY J. STROTHMAN

———

Russian Studies, 1972
Honorary Doctor of Humane Letters, 2008
Secretary, 1998 –2008
Trustee, 1990 – 1996
Fellow, 1997 – 2008

MOREHOUSE
C O L L E G E

WALTER E. MASSEY
President

May 21, 1996

Mr. Henry Sharpe, Jr.
Brown University
Corporation Office
Box 1887
Providence, RI 02912

Dear Henry:

By now, I must be an expert at writing letters of resignation from the Board and the Corporation of Brown University. I resigned after my term as Trustee and again when I had to leave the Fellows to become director of the National Science Foundation. I sincerely appreciate the Board's invitation to return to serve out my final year as a member of the Board of Fellows. I apologize that I have not been able to contribute as much as I would have liked during this final year. My new duties as president have simply absorbed my time more than I thought.

I have always taken pride in being one of the few non-alumni members of the Board of Trustees, and especially the Board of Fellows. I have been associated with Brown University for almost thirty years -- in practically every position the University offers: as faculty member, administrator, and member of the Board. This is far longer than I have been associated with either of my alma maters! So, it is clear that I have a very strong affection for this institution.

Through my service at Brown, I have established life-long friends among the faculty, students, alumni, and Corporation members. I have also learned a great deal through my interactions and experiences at Brown. I would not have been able to achieve many of the things of which I am so proud had I not had the opportunity to learn from individuals at this great institution.

I do not intend for my resignation from the Board to sever my relationships with Brown. I intend to take the title Fellow and Trustee Emeritus very seriously. You will see Shirley and me on many occasions, and we look forward to being able to contribute in whatever modest ways we can to the future health of Brown University. It is with a sense of poignancy, and I must say pride, that I submit my resignation for the third time from this august body.

Sincerely yours,

Walter E. Massey

830 Westview Drive, S.W., Atlanta, Georgia 30314-3773 • (404) 215-2645

Walter E. Massey

Honorary Doctor of Science, 1991

Trustee, 1980 – 1985

Fellow, 1985 – 1990, 1995 – 1996

Aquila Management Corporation

380 Madison Avenue, Suite 2300, New York, N.Y. 10017   (212) 697-6666

January 29, 1996

Mr. Henry D. Sharpe, Jr.
Secretary of the Corporation
Brown University
Providence, Rhode Island 02912

Dear Henry,

As I realize that my six year term as an active Trustee of the University is nearly over, and as I ponder my resignation letter, I keep recalling the theme of the song recorded by Peggy Lee - "Is That All There Is?"

And, in doing so, I find myself reviewing my years of involvement with Brown.

About 20 years ago, when I was invited to be a Director of the Brown Football Association, I was asked to raise $250,000 to help redo parts of the stadium. Through "Operation Pride," we replaced the bottom-splintering seats with new aluminum ones. Once that was accomplished, the high activity level was replaced by a pause and a big void. And, the refrain, "Is That All There Is?" came over me.

Then, a few years later, I was asked to be President of the Brown Club of Fairfield County, Connecticut to help build higher alumni participation. Four years later, after creating an increased favorable awareness for Brown in the area and a significantly higher level of alumni involvement, my term was up. Again, the big void set in. And, there was that refrain, "Is That All There Is?"

Several years later, the pause in involvement was interrupted by my nomination and election as President of the Associated Alumni. What followed was a very demanding, time-consuming, yet exceptionally rewarding adventure. Then, the term expired and again a big quiet period descended. And, again, the thought emerged, "Is That All There Is?"

Then, along came the nomination and election by the alumni of me as a Trustee. What an honor and thrill! The participation and experience have been most gratifying. The past six years have just flown by. And, now along comes that thought again, "Is That All There Is?"

But, now, though, further realization emerges. It is **not** all there is." If one is willing to spend the time and energy on behalf of this great University, another opportunity will arise.

Where will the next call come from? Who can predict? But, sure enough, I know it is out there.

And, for a guy like me who attended Brown on a NROTC scholarship and worked as a dormitory proctor and waiter to pay for room and board, whatever call it might be will provide additional great gratification and rewards. It will be another opportunity to give something back for the benefit of the rising generations.

And, so, with this resignation letter, I do not say "Good-bye" - but rather, "Au revoir."

In Deo Speramus - until we meet again - dear old Brown.

Sincerely,

Lacy B. Herrmann '50
Chairman and Chief Executive Officer

Aquila Management Corporation

Lacy B. Herrmann
Economics, 1950
Trustee, 1990 – 1996

To have shared rewarding, middle-aged
kaleidoscopic days with my fellow trustees
has been an honor and a pleasure.

—GEORGE L. BALL

———

Economics, 1960
Trustee, 1982 – 1987

J. Carter Brown

Director Emeritus, National Gallery of Art

May 5, 1998

Dear Hank:

The time has come, as the end of my term approaches, for me to submit my resignation as a trustee of Brown.

It would have been a privilege at any time to serve this extraordinary university; but having had the opportunity to march under the banner of Vartan and Artie, and then to be involved in the search process, and to see the new team come out on to the field with so much savvy and verve, makes me burst with pride to be able to claim that I am in any way a Brunonian.

Although I grew up playing on the Green three blocks from my home, for years I considered myself more or less an outsider. It has thus been of enormous personal satisfaction to be part of this fabulous institution as it leaps from strength to strength.

Thank you for including me.

Sincerely,

J. Carter Brown

Mr. Henry D. Sharpe, Jr.
Secretary
Brown University
Box 1887
Providence, Rhode Island 02912

1201 PENNSYLVANIA AVENUE, N.W., SUITE 621, WASHINGTON, D.C. 20004
TELEPHONE (202) 347−1906 TELEFAX (202) 347−2107

J. Carter Brown
Honorary Doctor of Laws, 1970
Trustee, 1992 – 1998

May 18, 2022

Chancellor Samuel M. Mencoff
Secretary Richard A. Friedman
President Christina H. Paxson
Brown University
Corporation Office Box 1887
Providence, RI 02912

Dear Sam, Rich, and Chris,

I am somewhere high over the Atlantic Ocean heading west to NYC in the middle
of the night. When I land, this letter is due. The combination of composing a letter
I never really wanted to write and my natural ability to procrastinate accounts for
the circumstances. I generally complete tasks on time, but not a moment too soon.
Apparently, I am consistent. This is how I made my way through Brown 45 – 49
years ago . . . cramming, working at wee hours of the night, and always last minute.
Truthfully, I did not learn these bad study habits at Brown; I just honed them there. My
acknowledged flaws were apparent at a much earlier age. And that brings me to a very
important point about my feelings about Brown. Simply, I feel deeply indebted to Brown
for accepting me and educating me.

When I applied as a 16-year-old kid I could not have been mistaken for a strong
candidate. My high school experience was unusually short. I was rebellious and bored.
Those admissions folks either saw an underachiever that could be saved, or I just ended
up in the wrong pile. This letter will flow better if we go with the former. In short, Brown
made a bet on me a long time ago. For that I will always be grateful.

My Brown education was the foundation for lifelong learning. Vartan Gregorian said it
well when he talked about never really graduating because a "formal education is really
an introduction to learning where the skills to go on educating oneself are acquired and
inculcated into everyday life. You never graduate from life and hence never really graduate
from learning." What an enduring and life-changing gift Brown has provided me.

In 22 years as a Corporation member, I wrote one resignation letter. It was short. It was
not introspective. It was sincere. This feels very different, except for the sincere part.
This time my run has been much longer and my perspective is different owing to age.
In this 23-year span, the mostly exogenous challenges we faced at the Corporation were
seismic—two recessions, multiple wars, extreme and persistent social injustices, crazy
political division, a climate crisis, and a once-a-century pandemic. And despite these
headwinds, Brown has thrived. Brown is in a much better place—in absolute and relative

terms—today than when I joined the board in 2000. I did not have much to do with Brown's success, but I had a ringside seat, inspired by our leaders and learning from my colleagues. Two presidents, three chancellors, and this body of trustees should take a bow for our successes during this quarter-century run.

The shared responsibility of the Corporation Members to guide the University unites us. The stakes are high . . . we are responsible for a 257-year-old institution of higher learning and research. The impact of our work is profound. We do it for love, obligation, or just because the effort for the noble and far-reaching goals of the University is worth it. And our different perspectives are exactly why the Corporation works so well. We reflect the large group outside our meeting room that we hope to elevate through knowledge.

I am grateful for the friendships made or sustained among the over one hundred Corporation members that I have been privileged to work with. I hope those continue. I am confident that this consistently engaged and smart group will continue to make the right, difficult decisions. I feel extremely lucky that my tenure coincided with Chris's Presidency and Ruth's before her.

Chris's exceptional management skills and logic, matched only by her ability to connect with people, are the foundation of her significant achievements already as President. My term also coincided with three outstanding chancellors that shared a love and commitment to Brown. I have complete trust in Sam; that comes easily. Moreover, I am delighted to see the kid in front of me in seventh grade end up again with me in a school room over 50 years later. How improbable is that.

Three terms and two resignation letters later, I am still grateful to Brown . . . for letting me through the gates and fostering in a young boy a love of learning that still burns brightly.

Landing now.

With appreciation and respect,

Jonathan

———

Jonathan M. Nelson
Economics, 1977
Trustee, 2000 – 2006, 2007 – 2011
Fellow, 2011 – 2022

May 2021

Dear Rich (and all of you),

I just celebrated my 50th reunion. Looking back to my graduation 50 years ago, I remember seeing alumni who had come back for their 50th. They seemed so OLD to me—and I guess I was surprised that they loved Brown enough to still be connected after all those years. Now I understand that so much better—as I reflect on how central Brown was in shaping the person I am now.

It was at Brown that I first learned about community organizing by participating in the effort to implement the New Curriculum. It was at Brown that I learned to take intellectual risks. It was at Brown that I learned about the connection between the spiritual and the political. In fact, I gave my first sermon at Brown, in the Baptist Meeting House! I was one of the two students elected by our class to give a baccalaureate speech. I didn't know it was a sermon at the time—but, in retrospect, that is exactly what it was. It ended with these words: "When women demand to be treated as human beings, they are threatening the fabric of a society which objectifies all of its people. It is not sufficient to 'liberate' women into such a society; in fact, true liberation, in those terms, is impossible. The women's movement, the Black movement, and the anti-war movement are all part of the same struggle—the struggle to reshape our society so as to make people whole. This is the world we are graduating into; this is the world we have to change."

A teacher in seminary once told me that a rabbi only preaches one sermon in his or her life—and I guess it's true. I've been preaching versions of the same sermon ever since, and working with other people to reshape society to make people whole. It was Brown that gave me the tools and the chutzpah to be part of the work.

One of the many gifts of being first an Alumna Trustee and then a Fellow has been the opportunity to continue to learn. I've learned so much about leadership from the astonishing presidents I have been privileged to work with, first Ruth Simmons and now Chris Paxson. As we all know, Chris's vision, clarity, skill, and ability to create and support her breathtaking team has led us through one of the most challenging periods in our country's history. Over all these years on the Corporation, I learned how institutions can become more effective if they are willing to challenge "the way we always did things" and ask instead "how can we do our work better." It has been such a stimulating and exciting time to be part of the Corporation as Brown has continued to reimagine itself, confronting the difficult challenges of its historic complicity in structural racism, taking sustainability so seriously, seizing the opportunity to become a truly diverse and inclusive community, and building on Brown's unique distinctiveness.

All of you have been my teachers.

I am particularly grateful to Russell Carey who was the staff to Campus Life when I was Co-Chair years ago, to Barbara Chernow who helped make Audit and Risk comprehensible to me, and to Catherine Pincince and Amalia Davis whose care for me was without measure. And I was not the least surprised when I participated in exit interviews with former trustees and learned that what they valued most was the connections they made with others on the Corporation, the senior team, and the staff. They all told me that they hoped those connections would continue to be part of their lives. That is also true for me.

Rabbis end their sermons (and even letters) with blessings. Here is mine. In Jewish tradition, when one book of Torah concludes and another begins, you say; "Hazak Hazak V'yitchazek: From strength to strength, may we strengthen each other." With much gratitude to Brown and to all of you for strengthening me, may Brown continue to grow from strength to strength.

With boundless thanks,

Laura Geller '71

———

Laura Geller
Religious Studies, 1971
Trustee, 2001 – 2007
Fellow, 2010 – 2021

12 words for 12 years

April 29, 2019

Dear Rich,

I hereby submit with regret my resignation from the Brown University Corporation.

Sincerely,

Joan Wernig Sorensen

———

Joan Wernig Sorensen
Psychology, 1972
Honorary Doctor of Humane Letters, 2019
Trustee, 2006 – 2012, 2013 – 2019
Fellow, 2020 – 2028

I am impressed with the individuals on this Board—who
are uniquely talented, accomplished, yet warm and
genuine and connected in their mutual love for Brown.

— ZACHARY J. SCHREIBER

International Relations, 1995
Trustee, 2016 – 2022

Members of the Corporation of
Brown University, 2022

"Gentlemen this day Nov 23 1788 . . .

. . . I hope to see Providence
but it is not Likely that Ever it will be
so—old age and infirmities have overtaken
me—I was born in the year 10 and
next march am 79 years old—Gentlemen
you cannot show me more respect or have
more good wishes for me than I have
for you and the whole Corperation:
God bless you, and prosper you all
in all your honest Endeavours to
maintain the Credit and Reputation
of your College"

Reverend Edward Upham
Corporator of The College
Honorary Master of Arts, 1769
Fellow, 1764 – 1788

II 141
141

Gentlemen this day, Nov 23 1788
I received your Letter of Sep 5th it was
Caryed to Northampton and was theare
neare 2 months before it came to hand
+ Otherwise I shold have been glad to have
been with you — youre Letter came two
Late. I suppose, beause, you directed it
to Northampton when it shold have
been, Superscribed, WestSpringfield —
Northampton is more, then 24 miles
from my Dwelling place — I am Sorey
Gentlemen that you, or the Corporation
Shold meet with the Least dificulty
upon my account — you have Shone me
too much respect, in that, you have not
Long before now Chosen a better man
In my place — I pray you all to do it
Immediately — I hope to see Providence
but it is not Likely that ever it will be
So — Old age and infirmities have overtaken
me — I was born in the year 10 and
next march am 79 years old — Gentlemen
you Cannot show me more respect or have
more good wishes for me then I have
for you and the whole Corporation:
God Bless you, and prosper you, all

in all your honest Endeavours to
maintain the Credit and Reputation
of your College ——————

I am Gentlemen your Sincere
friend and humble Servant
Edward Upham

Index

First Name	Last Name	Graduation Year	Resignation Year	Page
ChiChi	Anyoku	2014	2019	60 – 61
Thomas B.	Appleget	1917	1963	15
Isaac	Backus	—	1799	24 – 25
Bernicestine McLeod	Bailey	1968	2007	22 – 23
George L.	Ball	1960	1987	156
Craig E.	Barton	1978	2019	63
Andrea Terzi	Baum	1983	2016	88 – 89
Sarah Morse	Beardsley	1918	1963	91
Brian A.	Benjamin	1998	2021	57 – 58
Thomas W.	Berry	1969	2002	31
George H.	Billings	1972	2017	147 – 148
Sophia Schaffer	Blistein	1941	1976	86 – 87
Amanda T.	Boston	2016	2021	145 – 146
Allyn L.	Brown	1905	1963	102, 103
Bette Lipkin	Brown	1946	1975	79
Daniel L.	Brown	1912	1963	112
J. Carter	Brown	—	1998	157
John	Brown	—	1803	136 – 137
Nancy L.	Buc	1965	2004	94
Vincent J.	Buonanno	1966	1991, 2004	3, 124
J. Scott	Burns, Jr.	1969	2003	128
Kate	Burton	1979	2015	122
Gordon E.	Cadwgan	1936	1966	17, 104
Marvyn	Carton	1938	1987	17, 18
Alison K.	Cohen	2009	2015	9
Sally Hill	Cooper	1952	1984	96
Joel	Davis	1956	1973	67

First Name	Last Name	Graduation Year	Resignation Year	Page
Joseph L.	Dowling, Jr.	1947	1985	129
Ruth Burt	Ekstrom	1953	1988	xvii – xviii, 83
José J.	Estabil	1984, 1988	2019	51 – 52
Christine Dunlap	Farnham	1948	1981	99
Todd A.	Fisher	1987	2019	59
Timothy C.	Forbes	1976	2009	101
Laura	Geller	1971	2021	160 – 161
Peter B.	Green	1980	2003	144
Michael P.	Gross	1964	1992	107
Cathy Frank	Halstead	—	2017	39
John J.	Hannan	Parent 2010, 2014, 2014	2017	38
Alan G.	Hassenfeld	—	1996	113
Galen V.	Henderson	1993	2009	40 – 41
John B.	Henderson	1946	1990	120 – 121
Lacy B.	Herrmann	1950	1996	154 – 155
Elie	Hirschfeld	1971	1999	10
Donald C.	Hood	1968, 1970	2017	19
Jean E.	Howard	1970	1981	119
Pauline Barrows	Hughes	1921	1967	92
Dorsey M.	James	1983	2015	53
Paul H.	Johnson	1958	1977	125
Steven R.	Jordan	1982	2009	16
Artemis A. W.	Joukowsky, Jr.	1955	2009	142 – 143
Elizabeth Goodale	Kenyon	1939	1970	81
Noritake	Kobayashi	Parent 1985	1997	20 – 21
Benjamin V.	Lambert	1960	1989	74
Marie J.	Langlois	1964	2007	105
Debra L.	Lee	1976	2001	65
Robin A.	Lenhardt	1989	2019	5 – 7
Fredrick	Lippitt	—	1970	70
W. Duncan	MacMillan II	1953	1979, 1994	45, 110 – 111
Hunter S.	Marston	1908	1960	34
Walter E.	Massey	—	1996	153
Elliot E.	Maxwell	1968	1977	29 – 30
Divya	Mehta	2018	2023	43 – 44
Samuel M.	Mencoff	1978	2009	69
Margaret Conant	Michael	1951	1986	130
Kevin A.	Mundt	1976	2017	54

First Name	Last Name	Graduation Year	Resignation Year	Page
Srihari S.	Naidu	1993, 1997	2019	27
Nancy Fuld	Neff	1976	2016	150 – 151
Jonathan M.	Nelson	1977	2022	158 – 159
Viet	Nguyen	2017	2020	35
Claiborne	Pell	—	1979	42
Elizabeth Jackson	Phillips	1945	1978	36, 37
Steven	Price	1984	2017	126 – 127
Doris Brown	Reed	1927	1974	71
Mya L.	Roberson	2016	2019	62
Steven	Robert	1962	2012	135
Carmen M.	Rodriguez	1983	2011	117 – 118
Thomas E.	Rothman	1976	2015	115
Charles M.	Royce	1961	2013	49
Eileen M.	Rudden	1972	2009	55
Robert P.	Sanchez	1958	1999	108
Zachary J.	Schreiber	1995	2022	163
Darius	Sessions	—	1785	46 – 47
Henry D.	Sharpe, Jr.	1945	1999	131 – 133
Barbara Mosbacher	Smullyan	1945	1974	109
Joan Wernig	Sorensen	1972	2019	162
Anita V.	Spivey	1974	2004	32 – 33
John	Stanford	—	1789	ix
Wendy J.	Strothman	1972	2008	152
Edward	Sulzberger	1929	1972	68
Eugene C.	Swift	1942	1971	75
O. Rogeriee	Thompson	1973	2005	93
Thomas J.	Tisch	1976	2022	12 – 14
Preston C.	Tisdale	1973	2021	72
Edwin H.	Tuller	1935	1969	8
Edward	Upham	—	1788	164 – 165
Jerome C.	Vascellaro	1974	2021	139
Jean MacPhail	Weber	1954	1988	95
Augustus A.	White III	1957	1992	140 – 141
Judith Cameron	Whittaker	1959	1982	90
Ruth Harris	Wolf	1941	1977	84 – 85
Frank M.	Yatsu	1955	1974	106
Lauren	Zalaznick	1984	2017	xi – xv, 171 – 173

Acknowledgments

BROWN IS A MODEL of scrupulous respect for academic freedom. The Corporation's leaders, President Christina H. Paxson and Chancellor Samuel M. Mencoff 1978, held this book to their high standard of discerning intelligence. Their support helped me evolve an optimistic hypothesis into a valuable part of Brown's history. During the most tumultuous period in recent memory, each always had time for me.

I want to thank everyone involved in bringing this book to fruition. Especially every current and former trustee and fellow who has given their "wisdom, work, or wealth" so generously. The letters selected for inclusion in this volume leave out a significant number of truly memorable and enlightening stories of personal growth and service to Brown. It is evident that each author truly embodies "a life of usefulness and reputation."

I'm certain that I'm not the only person who had this idea. To each of you, I hope this book aligns with your highest expectations.

Catherine Pincince, the Senior Associate Secretary of the Corporation of Brown University, has been my partner since the project's inception. The details of this book are nearly infinite. Catherine worked tirelessly. She guided me through a maze of Brown's internal pathways. An archival sleuth, she ferreted out letters, documents, and data from all corners of the campus and beyond. And for her mastery of the devil called Google Drive, I am indebted.

Russell Carey, Executive Vice President for Planning and Policy at Brown, has comprehensive historical and institutional knowledge of the University. Through him, my understanding of the history of Brown and the Corporation and its governance informed many aspects of the book and substantially enriched my knowledge.

Logan Powell, Associate Provost for Enrollment and Dean of Undergraduate Admission, fundamentally helped me develop my curatorial process.

Cass Cliatt, Senior Vice President for Communications, and Nicole Picard, Associate General Counsel, gave essential guidance from start to finish.

Thanks to Jennifer Betts, Assistant Director for The John Hay Library and University Archivist; Raymond Butti, Senior Library Expert, Special Collections, Archives; Lindsay Elgin, Senior Library Technologist, Special Collections; and Nick Dentamaro, Communications Photographer, for facilitating our mountain of research requests. It was an honor to pore over the material in the grand yet accessible library and archive.

A number of people lent their time, expertise, opinions, and support: Andrew Blauner 1986, Jeff Eugenides 1982, Russell Fine 1985, Monica Halpert, Barbara Heller 1984, Jonathan Karp 1986, Susan Margolin 1984, and Grace Miller 2024, who painstakingly transcribed the eighteenth- and early-nineteenth-century manuscripts; Jane Olson, David Perlmutter 1984, Alex Schwartz, B. Z. Schwartz, Wendy Strothman 1972, Robert Zalaznick, and Barbara Zakin 1984. And deepest thanks to Richard Fishman, Professor Emeritus of Visual Art 1965 – 2018, for first bringing me back into the Brown fold.

My fellow human Dr. Augustus White III 1957 engaged in numerous conversations about the state of the world, including his many "firsts" during his thirty-plus years of dedication to Brown and the Corporation.

Ruth Burt Ekstrom 1953 is a pioneer who prefaced this book with a strong sense of history but without the distorting lens of nostalgia.

Former Chancellor Thomas J. Tisch 1976, LHD 2022 hon., graciously shared an encyclopedic knowledge of Brown and its dramatis personae on numerous occasions. In addition, I am grateful to him for originally encouraging me to put my name on the ballot as a potential Elected Trustee. This cohort continues to be an essential constituency of the Corporation.

I am most grateful to our Readers Council, a group of trustees and fellows who took on the most crucial task, the assessment of the letters themselves. Each devoted a significant amount of time they surely did not have. Their breadth of perspective shaped the book: Bernicestine McLeod Bailey 1968, LHD 2023 hon.; Andrea Terzi Baum 1983, who always goes the extra mile; Mark Blumenkranz 1972, MD 1975, MMSc 1976; Amanda Boston AM 2016, PhD 2018; Nancy L. Buc 1965, LLD 1994 hon., especially for her dedication to and respect for language that accurately reflects the history of women's education at Brown; Brickson Diamond 1993; Laura Geller 1971; Dorsey James 1983, my inspiration for this book, a friend, and a person who matters; Peige Katz 1991; Carlos Lejneiks 2000; and Srihari Naidu 1993, MD 1997.

This was not an easy book to publish. Jonas Kieffer 2005 at West Wing Writers donated his editorial prowess and, moreover, his friendship. At Disruption Books, Sheila Parr created this dignified design, which enhances rather than distracts from the words on the page. And Kris Pauls, my editor and publisher, who quickly absorbed "the Brown way" and steered this novice through every phase of the editorial and production processes up against daunting deadlines with gentle expertise.

To my family of English concentrators: Ada Dolan-Zalaznick 2017, Lucy Dolan-Zalaznick 2019, and Dale Dolan-Zalaznick 2024. They encouraged me to do the hard work. Their textual and visual acumen is hard to keep up with. And to Phelim Dolan 1985, the true scholar and aesthete of the family, who has indulged my purple prose since we met on the Brown campus almost forty-five years ago. The collective D-Z wisdom and our unique Brown experiences make this book, and my world, better.

And to my parents—for letting me do it all, always.

Thank you.

Lauren Zalaznick, Editor

Credits

Resources

The Brown Alumni Magazine

The Brown Daily Herald

The Brown University 250th Anniversary Timeline

The Brown University Historical Catalogue

The Brown Digital Repository

The Brown University Website

The 1945 Edition of the Charter of Brown University with Amendments and Notes

The History of Brown University, by Reuben Aldrich Guild, Librarian of the University, 1869

The John Hay Library and Archives

The Pembroke Center Archives and Oral History Project

Images

xv: Courtesy of Lauren Zalaznick

xvi: Photograph Collection, Brown University Archives

xviii: Brown University Archives

2:    Photograph Collection, Brown University Archives

11:   David Macaulay

17:   John Forasté, Photo Collection, Brown University Archives

23:   John Forasté, Photo Collection, Brown University Archives

26:   John Forasté, Photo Collection, Brown University Archives

36:   Brown University Archives

48:   Nick Dentamaro / Brown University

On the cover:

About the Editor

LAUREN ZALAZNICK has devoted her career in media to transforming the cultural landscape. Zalaznick has received many honors for her achievements, including two Peabody Awards and numerous Emmy Awards. *TIME* magazine named her one of the "TIME 100: World's Most Influential People" and she was the subject of a *New York Times Magazine* cover story. Zalaznick's interviews have been archived at the Television Academy Foundation and the Smithsonian. Her TED Talk, "The Conscience of Television," has been viewed and shared close to a million times. Zalaznick graduated with a degree in English from Brown University in 1984, magna cum laude and Phi Beta Kappa, and is a trustee emerita. She currently lives and works in New York City.

About the Type

This book is set in Freight Text and Ageo. Freight Text is a serif typeface created by American font designer Joshua Darden in 2005. Inspired by eighteenth-century Dutch typefaces, Freight Text is expressive, warm, and elevated. Ageo is a soft geometric sans serif font family created by Indonesian font designer Eko Bimantara in 2019. This typeface blends Bauhaus and modern styles for a clean look that is both elegant and offbeat.